MW00953781

52 SALES QUESTIONS ANSWERED

SCOTT SAMBUCCI

Copyright © 2013 Scott Sambucci

All rights reserved.

ISBN-13: 978-1484916353

DEDICATION

To Everyone

CONTENTS

Preface

This book is a composite of answers to these questions from various sources. For the past few years, I've been answering questions by clients in workshops, personalized advisory sessions, and via email. On Quora (find me here: http://www.quora.com/Scott-Sambucci), random strangers ask me to answer questions all the time. The answers extracted from my Quora activity have been updated and expanded in many cases. In other cases, they are a cut-and-paste. This book is a compilation of answers to frequently asked questions.

I've organized the book so that each question is answered independently. That is, the book does not build on itself like many books with chapters. The reader should use the book frequently as a reference guide to difficult questions that arise during the workday. This also means from time to time, I may refer to a concept more than once or you may notice parts of one answer to be very similar to parts of other answers. Even with these occasional duplications, most of the content is original and does not overlap.

I've also organized the book as best I can into sections, so that groups of questions about the same major topic are together. Many times answering one question leads to more questions and this organization attempts to provide the reader with some flow, given the otherwise modular nature of the book.

Any references to outside resources, companies, blog posts, and books were done completely on my own and without request or provocation by these sources. I receive no financial gain for referring to these companies, except a reference or two to my other book I strongly urge you to buy and read, of course... (Check it out on Amazon: "Startup Sales: How to sell if you really, really have to and don't know how" found here: http://amzn.to/Nib6eX).

You might be asking, "Why 52 questions? Is this supposed to be one question per week?" I first thought about stopping at a nice round 50 questions. That number seemed too boring and unoriginal, so I added two more questions. Then, I was concerned that readers would relate "52" to weeks in the year, even though that was unintentional. Like a smart man, I ask my wife what I should do. She described this best: "When you're starting a company or a career in sales, questions arise all the time. If you can learn the answer to one of these questions every week for a year, your sales knowledge and abilities will increase so dramatically that you'll never need to worry about sales again." So there you have it – "52 Sales Questions Answered."

I think that does it for the formalities. Let's get to it now. If you have any questions about sales I haven't answered here, you can call or email me anytime at:

scott@salesqualia.com

(415) 596-0804

Prospecting & Lead Generation

What are the best ways to directly approach potential customers for a SaaS (Software-as-a-Service) app without being "salesy"?

First, a few tactical tips:

- **Look for registration names at industry conferences and events**. If nothing else, these events post the company names attending. You can call into the main number of these companies and ask for the department that is most relevant to your product. Go to the events, but avoid registration fees at all costs. There is plenty of "LobbyCon" you can do. It will be painfully obvious when it's time to actually pay to register. Don't feel bad about this.
- **Get to know the companies and people running the events.** Submit for speaking slots. You'd be amazed how many times they have speaker/panel needs, cancellations, and are searching for new perspectives on stale industry topics. It's a good way to get free registrations and appear knowledgeable.
- **Condense your demo to 5 minutes**, and then ask questions specific to the customer and her company.
- **Read industry publications.** Ask your prospect for their opinion about key industry topics. You'll be surprised how

this type of conversation unveils true customer sentiments and ultimately their product needs.

- **Get an iPad.** It reduces the psychological wall introduced by laptop clamshells and speeds up the "let me show it to you" transition.
- **Blog about your industry.** This will help your learning curve and it provides you content (and ultimately) value to share with prospective clients as you're developing your product and business.

There's a big difference between "selling" and being "salesy." Be very careful about avoiding the sale, because ultimately that's what you are trying to do. Every person you talk to is a prospective client, so treat him as such. If you are genuinely interested in solving a hard industry problem, your prospects will sense that and be willing to talk. If you appear to be only interested in gaining intelligence without offering anything value to the prospect, they'll view you as a time leech. Think about what value you can offer in return for these conversations.

Often this begins with gathering requirements from the customers. Yes, do this. Cautiously. If you haven't identified a critical business issue for your industry at the onset, then you don't have a product - you are a software consultant who creates custom solutions for each client.

At the enterprise level, every client has a different set of needs, so tailoring your product to a single client will be the kiss of death when you endeavor to sell more broadly. When a prospective client gives you a list of 50 things they'd like, there are only 2-3 that really matter - the rest are "nice to haves." You have to ask qualifying questions for each requirement and get to the critical business issue your prospective needs to resolve.

In these interviews speak in current terms - "The product does this..." or "The product solves this problem..." Speaking in current terms also teaches you how to sell your product and go for closes. If you speak hypothetically, this customer will give you a wish list, instead of telling you straight up if your product hits the mark.

A simple example -- you tell the prospective client your product has three (3) main functions. They reply, "That's great. Does is do #4?" Then, you ask, "Not yet, but if it did, are you ready to buy?" Additionally, taking the current approach allows you to go for a close, "So it sounds like the product solves a really big problem for you. Are you able to budget for this in your Q1 budget?"

Embrace the sales part of the conversation because ultimately, there are plenty of outstanding products that never take hold in the market because of the inability or unwillingness to sell at the early stages.

How do SaaS companies typically find their first six-figure customer?

Obviously, this depends on the market and product, but generally speaking, how do SaaS companies land that first "big sale" (which I've arbitrarily defined as $100K+ in annual revenue)? Is it through their personal networks? Cold calling? Trade shows? Something else?

I'd advise taking these routes:

1. **Network.**

    Most importantly, it is rarely going to be a first or second-level connection. You will probably need to work through several layers. For example, if you are selling a financial technology product for equity analysts and have a friend who is a trader at hedge fund, you'll need to go two or three deep to find a connection. Your friend might trade bonds, so he'll have to connect you with the equity trader at his fund who can then connect you with an equity analyst.

    The key point in the process is the equity trader. You can't depend on your friend to send him an email to forward to an analyst. You need to have a qualitative conversation with the equity trader, so she understands your product and can provide a resounding recommendation to her equity analyst contact. Otherwise, you won't get the meeting with the analyst. Treat every layer like a sale.

    Pro Tip #1: Never, ever assume someone will do the selling for you. You're friend my say, "Send me your presentation and I'll forward it to someone." Do the work yourself. Get the contact info and personally contact each person in the chain. Besides, they'll botch the message and won't be able to answer basic questions, which might derail the opportunity.

    Pro Tip #2: Send a handwritten thank you card to everyone along the way.

Pro Tip #3. Definitely use LinkedIn here.

2. **Conferences/Trade Shows.**

But... you need not attend. Simply go to the event website and find the speaker and attendee list. These people are inherently biased towards buying your new product. Why? Because they care enough about their jobs and professions to travel and interact to develop and share new ideas. (Not always the case, but more times than not.)

Use that as a call list. You can even say, "Hi Bill, I saw you're speaking at the Blah Blah Enterprise Software for the Cloud conference next month. Because I won't be attending, I'd like to share a few ideas with you either before or after the event related to your talk. Are you available on Tuesday for a call?" Bingo. Now, you're in a sales process with this person/company.

As a start-up, you need early adopters, plus these types of people are out circulating in the industry, which means you can use them as case studies and for references down the road when you hit the fat part of the market.

3. **Get a voice.**

Webinars, white papers, regular email drips, blog posts, emailing interesting news articles to the appropriate people on your contact list. This will generate conversation and showcase both your industry expertise and passion for the business.

4. **Alpha/Beta Testers.**

It sounds obvious, but I see lots of companies launch their product and then go look for customers. It seems like you'd want to have a little help assuring you're hitting the mark with your product to me.

Pro Tip #1. Proceed with caution. The product you build based on the specifications for Big Company Beta Tester may not be valid for the rest of the market. Keep selling and talking to the rest of the market, while you're developing the product around these beta test specs, so you're not stuck with a non-scalable sales or product development process.

Pro Tip #2: Have the terms of the beta test developed ahead of time - expectations, benchmarks, length of test, and conversion from 'beta' to 'paying.' It's easy to fall into a perpetual beta test mode. Twelve months later, your beta tester is still asking you to make changes without fronting a dime for development or a subscription while telling you, "Okay, so just make this one last change and then we can start paying..."

If possible, put this in a Work Agreement or Contract that requires their legal and vendor management approval. The end users might be able to try new products willy-nilly, but ultimately be unable to have a purchase approved. You may not always be able to do this upfront, if you can't have an agreed-upon plan during the beta test when the business side of the interaction will take place.

What are the typical top sources of customers for early-stage SaaS companies?

Where does the first $100k of revenue typically come from? How much of it is friends (or friends of friends)? Cold outreach to interested buys? Warm leads through inbound marketing?

Case #1: Altos Research

With Altos Research, the first $100k came from a combination of two separate product lines targeting different markets using the same core data platform. (For Real Estate agents, Altos has a $79/month subscription and for the Capital Markets, Altos sells data files to institutions and banks at a price point of $3k-10k+/month).

Many individual subscribers + one big enterprise sale = $100k

Individual Subscribers

The revenue resulted from simply hitting the phones to qualified leads and networking. The qualified leads were the hard part that took more than a year to develop. For the Individual Subscribers, I cannot underestimate the power of personally calling each registrant to the website, even though the product was "only" $79/month.

Our co-founder/CEO spent most of 2006 blogging about the real estate industry and connecting with other bloggers, while simultaneously developing the product. (This was 2006/pre-Twitter, when you had to write thoughtful posts and analysis about your business and industry...) This yielded some nice natural SEO traffic and inbound links from other industry bloggers. We also offered a free widget agents could place on their website which helped to promote the company.

We posted these same free widgets on the main company website for every real estate market across the country. Next to the live data, we posted a registration form that helped to qualify the inbound leads. After six months, there was pretty steady inbound traffic and 5-10 leads per day on the real estate agent side of the business. The live data aided tremendously with conversions.

From there, it was persistence with hitting the phones, contacting each registrant, asking about their business and how they found Altos Research, and then discussing how the product matched their needs. (Yup - plain old Sales 101.) Slowly, day-by-day and week-by-week, he accumulated about 75 individual real estate agent subscribers by the middle of 2007. Our conversion rate was about 10-15% of registrations to the website. This is why persistence was vital to the sale. Once we had qualified lead, it really was a numbers game - 10 calls led to a sale, but you just didn't know which one of the ten would buy.

The personal outreach was essential to gaining traction. While there was an auto-subscribe page for the product, we learned that even at $79/month, the product was considered expensive for an individual real estate agent. Once we had a conversation and showed them the entire product, their perception of price and value changed.

Capital Markets Revenue (a.k.a. "The Enterprise Sale")

The first client arrived via a network introduction. A professional friend suggested we present to another company he knew in our industry. The meeting went well and they became our first Capital Markets client within a few weeks. (This was VERY serendipitous, as we've learned over the next five years that a normal sales cycle for this clientele is closer to 6-12 months.) This first client had both an early-adopter mentality and the ability to take action. It wasn't until much later we realized this and why the network introduction was so powerful. The connector had to know this about the customer otherwise he would not have put us in touch.

Case #2: Aplia

Aplia is an educational software product for Economics professors (since purchased by Cengage Learning). We built a beta version of the product that ran automatically on the company website and started our outbound calling and emailing Economics professors, establishing need, showing the product demo, and gaining commitment.

This was back in 2002 by the way; the university market was a little trickier on the revenue side. While we "sold" the product to professors in the Spring, they didn't start using the product until the Fall semester and the students were the actual product purchasers at about $20 per user for the semester.

As a team, we divided the country into geographic territories and everyone called the universities on their list. Everyone became a sales person - our CEO, our tech admin, product manager, marketing manager - to grind through the list. Again, just darn hard work and persistence would develop traction with the first crop of early adopters.

I want to optimize the use of our contact lists in the long term; what is the state of the art for that?

I work in a very big company with dozens of products, we run many campaigns every year and I want to look at how best to share and manage these campaigns so that our customers aren't contacted many times uselessly, or become "contact weary". How?

Add value every time you contact your list. This means your outbound message, whether it be a phone call, personal email request, or marketing campaign must include useful content and ideas.

A few specific ideas:

- **"Top 5" Lists and Ideas** to help your targets improve their business. This is tactic used by bloggers for page view. Employ this same strategy in your outbound emails.
- **Offer free webinars around industry topics** your contacts will find interesting. This is NOT a webinar all about your product. For example, if you're selling biomedical devices you can plan a 15-minute webcast around proposed legislation and its potential effect on the biomedical industry, new innovations, or recent publications around related topics.
- **Summarize industry articles from unusual resources.** For example, if you're selling a CRM tool, find articles in places like Wired, Harvard Business Review, or Psychology Today that your contacts may not be reading every day. Bring new ideas and comment on how they relate to your customers to show your commitment to your industry.

Okay, so that covers the marketing angle. How you do you add value in sales calls? Ah…. This is a bit trickier. A few ideas:

- Reference recent industry articles relevant to your client and their practice.
- Share conference presentations and webcast announcements and recordings.

- Create connections and introductions for your prospect. Use LinkedIn introduce your prospect to someone else in the industry that might be interesting. (Be sure to get permission first before doing this.

Separately, on the structural side, establish tags in your CRM so that you have different lists based on who you contacted and why. There are several excellent plug-ins to Salesforce and email marketing tools that enable you to do this quickly. Then, send out emails on a regular schedule. If you're sending haphazardly, then prospects that do open your emails won't know when to look for your emails. Personally, I subscribe to four email newsletters that arrive to my inbox early AM. I read them every morning. Anything outside of that usually gets deleted or ignored because it comes in at times of the day when I'm not able to read them.

On the technical side, use an email marketing tool that enables you to track open rates and click-throughs so you can see how you're doing. Sounds basic, but too many companies "spray and pray." You have to know what's working. If you're consistently getting low open rates, then change your approach.

What are some rules of making successful follow up calls to prospects?

1. **Identify the difference between a "continuation" and an "advance."** (This is described in the book "SPIN Selling".[1]) An advance progresses the sale whereas a continuation simply maintains the sale in its current state.

   Example of an "advance":

   In an ***advance***, you talked with a prospect last week and you both agreed the prospect would talk with her team set up a product demo for everyone on her team. In your follow up call, you and prospect nail down a time ("next Tuesday at 10 am") and process for delivering the demo ("via WebEx").

   Example of a "continuation":

---

[1] Rackham, Neil, "SPIN Selling," (1988). Available on Amazom.com.

In this same scenario, a ***continuation*** would be a call to that same prospect and she tells you she's been really busy since your last call and hasn't had a chance to talk to the team. She asks you to try her again next week to talk then.

Alternately, a voicemail to your prospect is always continuation. The sales conversation is still open, but you're still in the same spot as you were following your initial call a week ago. (And remember to give yourself permission to call back!)

2. **Always prepare a script.** For even the simplest of calls, be prepared with exactly what you want to communicate. Be ready for every outcome:
    - You get voicemail.
    - You get the prospect's administrative assistant.
    - You get the administrative assistant's voicemail.
    - The prospect answers. He doesn't have time to talk and asks you to call back later today/tomorrow/next week.
    - The prospect answers. He doesn't have time to talk and tells you he will call you back later today/tomorrow/next week.
    - The prospect answers and has time to talk, but hasn't followed through with his action item from the last call, such as talking with his technical team about availability for a technical walk-through of your product.
    - The prospect answers, has time to talk and did talk to his technical team, but now they're not interested in your product.
    - The prospect answers, has time to talk, and he wants you to fly out for the technical demo on Thursday instead of running it by web meeting.
    - (Are you getting the picture?)

3. **Remember, in every conversation there is**:
    - What you want to say;

- What you think you say;
- What you do say;
- What the prospect hears;
- What the prospect remembers.

4. **Avoid ambiguity as to the reason for your call.** The lazy approach leads to non-action. For example, you've agreed to follow up via phone with a prospect.

   Lazy: You lead with "I'm calling to follow up on our call from last week..." This is weak and cedes control of the sales conversation.

   Strong: "We talked last week and I promised to gather more information about our product specs on the Wizz-Bang-Doo-Dad-ameter and you were going to check on budgets for the next quarter. I've got the product specs after sitting with our product specialist."

5. **Give yourself permission to call back again.** This is a big mistake I see often. You've talked to the prospect last week and agreed you would talk again this week.

   Wrong:

   > "Hi, this is Scott with ABC Software. We said we'd talk this week to discuss next steps. Give me a call when you have a chance at 415-555-1212..."

   Right:

   > "Hi, this is Scott with ABC Software. We said we'd talk this week to discuss next steps. Because I've missed you, I'll try you again this afternoon at 4 pm and if we don't connect today, expect a call at 8:30 am tomorrow. In the mean time, you can reach me at 415-555-1212..."

   The same principle applies in follow up emails. As you close your outbound email, give yourself permission to call again, "Thanks for your time. I'll give you a call on Friday morning at 10 am if you're not able to reply back to this email by then."

Check out Michael Pedone at Salesbuzz.com. He specializes in phone sales and techniques: http://www.salesbuzz.com/free-demo.

What are the sales materials typically required to close large enterprise software deals?

I'm thinking about all of the things that need to be created in order to have the best chance of closing a six-figure enterprise software deal. Examples might include a sales deck, a proposal template, and a contract. The company selling is a startup (approximately one year old, not well known yet in industry) and the solution is a SaaS product.

The external materials are pretty clear, presentations, contracts, and a description of your security information. All of these are very important (though I would argue strongly against a standard slide deck. More on this below...).

Let's instead focus on a few ***internal*** materials you'll need to develop B2B customers. These are designed to help you determine where you are in the sales cycle and take an objective appraisal on your close probabilities.

The "Where Am I in the Process" Worksheet

Print out this simple table for reference. Fill in a worksheet for each prospect and it will lead you to understand exactly where you are in the sales process with each. If you don't know the answers to all of the areas of the table, this alone could be the reason why you don't yet have the sale. Only after you know the key aspects of the process will you be able to address each.[2]

Competitor Grid

Through the product development and sales process, you've identified strengths and weaknesses of competitors. Document this on a one-page sheet so you and the sales team know what you're up against. For the enterprise sale, this is NOT a "how to handle such-and-such objection." It's a one-pager your sales reps can refer to as they plan their sales strategies with each client.

---

[2] This is based on the "Phases of the Purchasing Process" described in "Major Account Sales Strategies" (1989) by Neil Rackham. Available on Amazon.com.

Sales Question Tree

Every call is unique. However, the Question Tree forces your salesperson to begin each sales conversation with identifying the client's situation and developing a clear needs analysis. After making call after call over several months, it's all too easy for salespeople to begin running right to the end of the sales conversation without setting up the prospect properly. The Question Tree documents a clear path each unique prospect must take before reaching the payoff conversation and product walk-through.

Additionally, the Question Tree standardizes the sales process. Read this article at HBR.com by Mark Roberge, Senior Vice President of Sales at Hubspot:

"The Science of Building Scalable Sales Teams":

http://blogs.hbr.org/cs/2012/07/the_science_of_building_a_scal.html

So why do I say 'no' to a slide deck?

Presumably, your product is solving a very hard problem for your customers. A slide deck shows your prospects that all you do is puke on them with the same vomit you use with every other client even though you claim to be a solutions provider.

Why use a slide deck when you have a product? Have the customer join you for a presentation about the product. A slide deck is only a precursor to the product itself.

Online videos (under a minute in length) and white papers suggested by others do an excellent job of showcasing how keenly aware you are of the industry's problems.

The videos can highlight the major functionality in your product to generate interest in a full demo.

Anyone that says, "send me your PowerPoint deck and I'll circulate to our team", isn't a prospect. It's a polite way for the prospect to tell you they're not interested.

Managing the Sales Process

Business: In terms of sales, what are the three most important things to know about psychology?

1. **Bounded Rationality** - Articulated by Herbert Simon, 1978 Nobel Prize Winner for Economics.

   Organizations do not make optimal decisions, because they operate under the condition of imperfect information and individual biases. Simon referred to this as "satisficing."[3]

   When team managers attempt to reach consensus on a project, the decision process is fraught with pandering, or at a minimum, accounting for individual egos and incentives. If you've lost the sale of a good or service and thought - "How could they decide on company's XYZ's product? Ours is better, faster, and cheaper..." - you've likely experienced "bounded rationality" (assuming the analysis of "better, faster, cheaper" is indeed true). The internal discussion could have gone something like this: "We can do that, but how is John going to feel about it? Maybe instead we can go with Plan B. It's not as good but it will get the job done and appeases John."

---

[3] "Rational Choice and the Structure of the Environment," Psychological Review (1956).

Anyone working in an organization of any size has witnessed this concept in action; it is particularly evident as organizations grow larger. In an organization, as individual motivations converge at a decision point and access to information is limited (a.k.a. "imperfect information") suboptimal decisions frequently result. This also explains why Congress passes suboptimal laws with "pork barrel expenditures."[4]

In his paper, "A Behavioral Model of Rational Choice", Simon articulated the difference between "economic man", who theoretically decides rationally and optimally, and "administrative man", a servant of the organization ("organism") which suffers from imperfect information and individual biases.[5] From the paper:

> The apparent paradox to be faced is that the economic theory of the firm and the theory of administration attempt to deal with human behavior in situations in which that behavior is at least "intendedly" rational; while, at the same time, it can be shown that if we assume the global kinds of rationality of the classical theory the problems of internal structure of the firm or other organization largely disappear. The paradox vanishes, and the outlines of theory begin to emerge when we substitute for "economic man" or "administrative man" a choosing organism of limited knowledge and ability. This organism's simplifications of the real world for purposes of choice introduce discrepancies between the simplified model and the reality; and these discrepancies, in turn, serve to explain many of the phenomena of organizational behavior.

---

[4] Aiden Ward and Richard Veryard posted their very fine presentation to Slideshare - "Rationality and Decision-Making":
http://www.slideshare.net/RichardVeryard/rationality-and-decisionmaking.

[5] "A Behavioral Model of Rational Choice," The Quarterly Journal of Economics (1955).

In his 1978 Nobel Prize lecture entitled "Rational Decision-making in Business Organizations," Simon refers to the individuals' motivations as "subordinate goals":

> In organization theory it is usually referred to as subgoal identification. When the goals of an organization cannot be connected operationally with actions (when the production function can't be formulated in concrete terms), then decisions will be judged against subordinate goals that can be so connected. There is no unique determination of these subordinate goals. Their formulation will depend on the knowledge, experience, and organizational environment of the decision maker. In the face of this ambiguity, the formulation can also be influenced in subtle, and not so subtle, ways by his self-interest and power drives... Given a particular environment of stimuli, and a particular background of previous knowledge, how will a person organize this complex mass of information into a problem formulation that will facilitate his solution efforts?

2. **Risk Aversion & Loss Aversion -** These are two related concepts in economics and psychology.

> ***Risk Aversion:*** Individuals and organizations are risk averse, risk neutral, or risk loving, and in most cases, individuals and organizations are naturally risk averse, referring to the natural tendency to avoid risky situations and bets in most cases. This is why people buy insurance.
>
> As a salesperson, risk aversion can be overcome by identifying relative risk profiles of the decision team members in the target organization and developing a strategy map to adjust the positioning of your product and its affect to each individual. (Remember "Bounded Rationality" above - individuals within an organization have independent motivations and access to information.)

21

Mathematically, risk aversion is illustrated with a concave utility function:

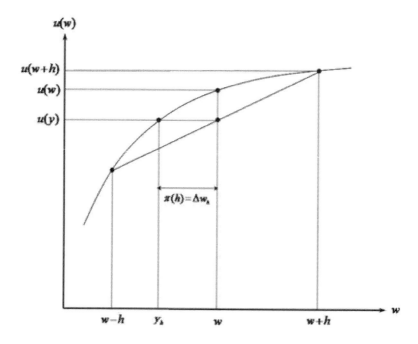

The graph shows the greater the risk's payout, the less usefulness (a.k.a. "utility") is realized by the individual or organization receiving the payout. While the potential outcome could be greater by taking more risk, the "utility" decreases as the outcome gain increases. In business, this explains why organizations rarely go for the "home run" outcome unless in a distressed state where downside risk is already mitigated by a deficient current state.

Managers overcome risk aversion by selecting risk-loving team members (if you can find them and know how to manage them) and providing the proper incentives to the team.[6] There is a body of academic and business literature on strategies for overcoming organizational risk aversion.[7]

---

[6] Think hard about you to motivate your team. Monetary incentives don't always work. Check out Daniel Pink's TED talk "The puzzle of motivation" found at:

Loss Aversion: Daniel Kahneman and Amos Tversky developed this concept as part of their work on "Prospect Theory." Loss aversion is an individual's preference to avoid a loss rather than make a gain. Kahneman won the Nobel Prize for Economics in 2002 despite never taking an Economics class. Tversky would likely have joined him but the Nobel committee does not award posthumously. Under loss aversion, individuals tend to act irrationally by taking larger gambles to avoid loss than they do to realize gains. When businesses make decisions based on this premise, it means status quo becomes more acceptable and change is only instigated when there is critical business issue that may result in a clear loss. Even if a product or service you are offering will "make this better", this is not as strong of an influence as a product or service that mitigates a pending loss.

You often hear of salespeople "selling fear." This is loss aversion in action. The salesperson is identifying a potential business loss and selling a service that will prevent the loss from occurring.

3. **Anchoring** - Kahneman & Tversky first described this concept in their 1974 article "Judgment Under Uncertainty: Heuristics & Biases."

Typically, "anchoring" is identified with pricing strategies. The "Manufacturer's Suggested Retail Price" (MSRP) posted to the car on the lot is an anchor. By setting an artificially high price in your mind, the dealer's willingness to drop the price from the MSRP during negotiations makes you feel like you have negotiated a good deal for yourself. You leave feeling satisfied for the price you paid and the dealer earns a tidy profit. This works even though

---

http://www.ted.com/talks/dan_pink_on_motivation.html.

[7] Start with this McKinsey Consulting Report: "Overcoming a bias against risk" by Tim Koller, Dan Lovallo, and Zane Williams (August 2012). Found online at: http://www.mckinsey.com/insights/corporate_finance/overcoming_a_bias_again st_risk.

both you and the car dealer know no one ever pays sticker price for a car. (If you have, I'm sorry. You got ripped off.) The mere action of posting MSRP price anchors you to a higher price at the onset of negotiations.

Anchoring is also powerful qualitatively. When interacting with your product for the first time, the prospect will develop an initial perception about your product and what it does. "Freemium" products can suffer from the anchoring effect, as users are introduced to the product's free version, become locked in, and then are asked to pay for additional functionality. Because the user is "anchored" to the notion that the product is free, there can be backlash or low conversion rates. Consider that Evernote has a 1/34 conversion rate from free to paid.[8]

Brands are also anchored by the market, though the anchor can be overcome - Hyundai and Subaru have done so over the last 20-30 years. Think about Hyundai's entrance to the US automobile market in the 1980's and their brand perception today. Remember these cars?[9]

Should I offer a free trial for my SaaS enterprise software? When I close the call after a product demo, there's often interest in the product so I schedule a follow up call for the next week. I don't offer a free trial if they don't ask for it. Is this the right approach?

If you have interest and engagement, a "free trial" would be warranted - just don't call it a "free trial." Instead, call it a "beta test" or something else that avoids the connotation of "free." If you are

---

[8] "Evernote Wants To Be The Automatic, Trusted Place To Store Your Life," TechCrunch (July 15, 2012). Found online at:
http://techcrunch.com/2012/07/15/evernote-libin-interview/.

[9] Kahneman recently published "Thinking Fast and Slow" that details Anchoring, Loss Aversion, and other psychological concepts for the non-economist.

allowing use of your product without a monetary exchange, you must generate a cost of some other kind with the user. When a prospect hears "free", that means they may or may not choose to use it, but it's okay if they don't because they incurred no costs.

Instead, under a "beta test", work with the user to determine 1-2 primary outcomes that would help them drive the decision-maker to a "yes." You need to focus them in on 1-2 outcomes, and avoid the temptation to teach the User Buyer to use every single wonderful feature of your product. I'm sure they're all great, but you need results to work towards commitment. Get your User Buyer to show real outcomes to their boss and express it in real dollars.

For example:

"Okay User, you said you aren't able to [INSERT THEIR DESIRED TASK] and if you could, [INSERT THE EXPECTED RESULT]."

"So I'll turn on your account and we'll focus on using [INSERT YOUR PRODUCT NAME] for that specific purpose. You said there are 5-10 of these incidents each day, so under this beta test, track the results. What do you think would be a reasonable increase in performance to make a case to your manager to purchase [INSERT YOUR PRODUCT NAME]?"

Then, hold your User Buyer accountable. If the response is something like:

"Let's wait and see how your software does and then we can revisit a purchase..."

"I'm not sure my manager would be willing to agree to that..."

"I'm not sure; let me get back to you..."

... then you don't have a serious sales prospect, or at least you know you don't have an influencer in the decision.

Additionally, analyze the sources and quality of your leads and prospects. Here are two questions to answer for yourself:

1. **Who are the Buyer Types you're speaking with?** If you are mostly speaking with "User Buyers," then a free trial may lead to an excited user, but you don't have engagement from the "Economic Buyer", the person that makes the purchasing decision.

2. **What are the sources of your leads?** Are these inbound leads or are you calling into the target companies? If these are inbound leads and most turn out to be User Buyers, consider changing your message and targeting to reach the Economic Buyers. This cuts the User Buyer "middle man" from the sale. This should speed up the process and result in higher conversion rates. (You may have fewer leads because there are fewer managers than users, so that's to be expected.)

What's the most effective method for "outbound" cold calls for SaaS products?

I've read Predictable Revenue and the author (Aaron Ross, who helped Salesforce build revenue in the early days) suggests you cold email exec-level people asking for intros to the right people. This seems to be effective, but I'm curious as to whether there are better ways to do "outbound" as a SaaS company?

I've read Aaron's book[10] and wouldn't label the cold emails to the company executives as "cold calls." These very specific emails are simply a hunt for information about the right person to contact in a target organization. You are not selling in these emails, nor is the intention to sell.

Now, when you are performing actual "cold calls"; instead label them "new calls" in your mind. It's an important mental model to use when approaching the call. This positions you as a peer having a conversation instead of the traditional sales mindset of "smiling and dialing" or "dialing for dollars." These antiquated approaches are fruitless and, more so, are just plain stupid with the amount of information easily available on LinkedIn, company websites, and personal networks.

With the amount of information available about individuals on LinkedIn, you can know quite a bit about the executive before the call. Additionally, research previous conference participation or speaking spots, papers or articles they've written, and quotes from news articles. In fact, executives expect you to know all of this about them before calling. If you call and start firing off very basic situation questions ("Are you the VP of Sales?") or information requests "Who is your target customer?", they'll be rather peeved and the call will end with, "Now's not a good time. Send me an email." And worse, unprepared sales calls like these give really smart, prepared salespeople like us a bad rap.

---

[10] Check out www.predictablerevene.com. I've read Aaron's book and found it very instructive.

SCOTT SAMBUCCI

I'm both a salesperson and an executive, so from time to time I receive inbound sales calls. When the person starts with something like, "Do you work in the housing market?" or "What type of work do you do in housing?", then we're done in 10 seconds. Had the person taken five minutes to Google me, the answers are blatantly obvious.

If you need a resource on effective outbound calling, Michael Pedone does a nice job of developing the right approach to these calls in his webinars (www.salesbuzz.com) with several free recordings on his site. One aspect he drives home is to approach the prospect with specific ideas on their business. You can warm up to this with good research or pre-selling by developing and sharing content/news articles/blog posts/white papers.

Now, once you have your "new call" targets figured out, prepare a Sales Call Map. An 11" x 14" paper is great for this. If you're a computer person, check out Mindomo, xMind, or Mindmeister (Google "mind mapping software") to draft electronically. The exercise is to think through the possible call paths. For example, when you dial the executive's number, the possible outcomes include:

1. Voicemail
2. Voicemail with an option to hit "0" for an attendant of extension "123" for her assistant
3. Voicemail with an out-of-office message
4. Voicemail with their cell phone number – "If you need to reach me right away, call me at 415-555-1212."
5. Assistant's voicemail
6. Assistant answers and the executive is out of the office
7. Assistant answers and the executive is in a meeting
8. Assistant answers and the executive is "unavailable"
9. Executive answers and seems rushed and unhappy that a salesperson is calling
10. Executive answers and says they are in a meeting and asks you to "call back later"
11. Executive answers and says they will call you back
12. Executive answers and asks you to send an email
13. Executive answers and is able to talk right now

14. Executive answers and tells you they are interested, but now's not a good time

Getting the picture? There are probably 5-10 more outcomes simply from dialing the executive's phone number. Think through these options and how you will address each and every situation. Write out your script for each, including a voicemail message (and your voicemail message should differ if you are transferred there by the assistant versus going direct to voicemail) for each option. Once you have your script prepared, practice it so you can speak it S-L-O-W-L-Y and C-L-E-A-R-L-Y, and so it sounds natural and not rehearsed.

Many cold calls fail simply because the salesperson fails to prepare. If you are sincere, professional, and customize your message, your percentages will increase markedly. Just remember the last time you received a call. When the person calling rushed through a script, you probably responded with – "Who is this and why are you calling?" – even though that's exactly what the caller told you when they called in the first place.

What's the best way to respond when a potential customer wants a longer free trial than you are willing to give?

We do a two-week free trial for our SaaS app and really want to hold to that length. Often we'll have a customer ask for a longer trial. While we can provide that, we don't want to in most cases. What's the best way to respond to this request?

My hunch is that when your prospects ask for an extension on their free trial, they tell you:

"I just didn't get to it because I was really busy."

This signals that:

- You failed to properly qualify the prospect and were so worried about making your sales vanity metrics look good, you turned on the free trial so you can tell everyone – "Yeah! We got a new user today!"
- You didn't create urgency or gain commitment from the prospect before the trial started.
- The prospect asked for a free trial because they were too nice to tell you they're not interested.
- The prospect doesn't really know why or how they'll use your product and they're hoping a free trial will magically help them see the light.

Which means you need to:

- Improve your situational analysis before starting the free trial.
- Create rules and expectations for your trial.
- Cut bait when your free trials are not willing to play by these rules.

Rules for your free trials:

1. **Reduce your trial to one week and start all free trial requests from the previous week at the same time.** Run your trials from Monday to Friday. Tell your prospects you

actively engage with your free trials and you can only support a certain number per week in order ensure their success.

2. **Mutually determine what you will measure and expected outcomes.** Set up the rules of trial so both sides have clear expectations. For example, let's say you're selling email marketing software. Determine the click-through and response rates AND gain commitment that if you meet these expectations, the prospect will buy your product. They may be a little wary of this, in which case you have more situational analysis to do.

3. **Schedule a 30 minute call to initiate the first login and confirm what 1-2 primary tasks you will accomplish.** With the email marketing software, have the prospect upload 100 contacts and construct an outbound email to send the next day.

4. **Do not share their login information with them until this call.** If they are unwilling to commit to 30 minutes with you to get started, what makes you think they'll spend any time looking at your product during the trial?

5. **Schedule a midweek status call.** This should be a clear deliverable. Using the email marketing example, your Wednesday call would be to review the results of the email campaign you built on Monday's initial call and the prospect sent on Tuesday.

Shut off your free trials at 5:00 pm on Friday, no exceptions. If they ask for another week, tell them, "Sure you can have as long as you would like with a subscription." Hold firm. If you really, really want to give in, then see rule #2; set expectations and gain commitment. Or you can tell your client your free trial cohort for next week is already full, but you can add them to a cohort two weeks from now.

What are some good ways to avoid asking dead end questions? How can I avoid getting short, yes/no answers?

If you manage the sales process question, there is no such thing as "dead-end questions", only dead-end conversations to the sales process because of lack of preparation.

To avoid dead-end questions (read: conversations):

1. **Maintain a 3:1 question ratio.** For every three (3) questions you ask, deliberately offer an opportunity for the prospect to ask a question and make a statement. Think of your interaction as a conversation, not an interrogation. This will markedly increase your prospect's interest and, further, their questions to you may often reveal more information to you than their answers to your questions. This can be extended to 4:1 based on receptivity of the prospect.

   For example, suppose you are selling project management software for the enterprise:

   Sales Question #1: "How many people in your organization are involved with the production of your XYZ product line?"

   Sales Question #2: "How is your team communicating project requirements to each other and deliverables along the way?"

   Sales Question #3: "What is the typical time line on your product development cycle? Is it a week, a month, several months, a year...?"

   Sales Question #4: "Do you guys think about speeding up the product development lifecycle, say as compared to identifying and implementing new features for a product? I was reading an article on Harvard Business Review about product development challenges and this seemed to be a pretty big push-pull for software product managers."

At this point, pause and allow the customer to ask you a question or two.

Notice that last question moves the conversation into a different direction. You are establishing credibility by mentioning the HBR article, plus now asking an opinion instead of a fact-based question. This requires the prospect to think and give their thoughts. Mostly importantly, as the call winds down later in the conversation, you can refer back to the HBR article:

> "I mentioned that HBR article earlier. I'll email it over to you. Lots of interesting perspectives you might like."

This is far and away better than just puking examples on him without confirming that cost savings matter to the prospect in the first place. And most importantly, this stemmed from the prospect pushing intelligence to you instead of you pulling out of them through your questioning strategy.

2. **Consider what your customer hears in your questions.** For example, if you really don't know if your prospect is using any project management software, then Question A is better than Question B:

A: "Are you using any project management software right now?"

B: "Which project management software are you using?"

Why? Because the open-ended version (Question B) can be received as condescending to the prospect. When you ask question B, the prospect might think - "What a brat. I've been managing projects at my company for 15 years with more than 10 people per project involved. We use Excel spreadsheets and email and have bootstrapped the company to a $20mln run rate." Consider the psychology of your questions, not just the information you hope to collect from them.

Question A allows you to follow up with "Which one?" or even better, Question C below.

If you're not sure if the prospect is using any project management software, then the best way to ask this question at the onset of the sales conversation is:

C: "How do you manage your projects now? Are you using any specific project management software, or a combination of tools like email and shared spreadsheets?"

This indicates earnest interest on your end as the salesperson to understand the prospect's situation and avoids the appearance you are attempting to track the prospect directly into a feature/benefits conversation about your product. If you ask Question C from the start, you'll be diving directly into the prospect's work flow process.

3. **Do your research.** If you need to ask a large number of yes/no questions, or are looking for creative ways to manufacture open-ended questions from yes/no questions, that probably means you haven't done enough leg work ahead of the sales call. The prospect will become bored very quickly because all of these types of questions (defined by "situational" questions in the SPIN Selling method) only benefit you, the salesperson. Meanwhile, the prospect might be sitting there wondering when you're planning to start hammering him about your products or services.

    For example, if my target prospect just spoke at a Project Management Software conference and their presentation discusses how they love using competitor's ABC software, you shouldn't be asking, "So.... what software are your using now? Do you like it?"

4. **Never assume.** Say the prospect tells you they are using ABC software, which many of your current customers have converted from because of a particular weakness. Do NOT assume this customer has the same problem.

For example, suppose ABC software (your competitor) is only available as an install on a local system vs. your XYZ software which is web-based. The prospect tells you - "We're using ABC software." Do NOT assume this is deficiency with this particular customer. Perhaps the users for this customer purposely do not have Internet access on the terminals where this software is used for security reasons and is a condition the prospect prefers. Always qualify each condition.

If you wrongly assume the local install condition is a negative for the customer, this will immediately lead to a dead-end to the conversation because 1) you look like a doofus for failing to collect enough information about the prospect's situation and decision criteria, and 2) now you'll be back-tracking and hunting for another reason to have the prospect check out your software, and the prospect knows it. You've ceded control of the conversation to the prospect out of arrogance. Remember, what "assume" spells.

I have no clue about enterprise sales, but I met a bunch people from big companies, who are interested in my product. How do I figure out what to do?

I've been building a startup, and I thought I'd target smaller companies, but I went to a conference, and met a few people from some major companies, who seem really interested in what I'm doing. I'm not entirely sure how they will use it, but it seems to make sense and fit into their current strategy. Should I hire a salesperson? How do I figure out how to pursue this?

In the short term, the most important step is immediate and persistent follow up with these leads. You'll find that if had 5-10 good conversations, 1-2 or will end up being immediate targets for you. That's just the way it is. Don't take this personally. Conferences put people in a creative, active frame of mind. When they get back to their offices, it's back to putting out fires.

Know that:

- **The person you met may not be the decision-maker in the larger organization.** Many large companies have highly specialized roles like Community Manager, Product Evangelist, or Technology Implementation Manager. These types of people are the ones who attend conferences to identify market trends, find new applications for their product, or to identify company partners. They can be senior-level individuals without a staff, budget, or purchasing authority. They often love new ideas to hard problems, like the one your product tackles. But they simply are the wrong people. They want to keep in touch because it's their job to know about companies like you, but they can't buy your product and might not even know who the right person would be to talk with at their company.

- **The person you talked with forgot who you were 30 minutes after the conversation.** So many times I've been to conferences and held a 30-minute conversation at a trade booth with a prospective client. The conversation was great. We really hit it off. We talked about our kids and triathlons and how we both love Austin. The product looked like a great fit for his company. The next day at lunch, I saw this person in the lunch buffet line and he looked at me blankly when I said, "Hey Bob, how's the conference!" It just happens.

- **The person you talked to may not be in charge of the division or group that ultimately needs your product.** For example, let's say you're selling Enterprise-level Project Management software that enables the sales team to monitor engineering progress. Sounds great to the Sales Manager you talked to at the conference - "We really need that!" But ultimately the Engineering team is responsible for choosing, implementing, and paying for project management software. The Sales Manager didn't act out of malice, they just don't have direct decision power.

Be direct and persistent with your follow up. Use the phone, and follow up with an email. Then, use the phone again two days later. You have to find which of the 5-10 are really hot to trot right now.

Prepare a set of situational questions for the prospect and use the phone to get this information. For example:

- **What is their current process and how did that process come to be?** Big companies are laden with dumb, stupid, onerous, illogical processes. And they hate to change them. INDIVIDUALS within the big company may want them to change, but when the change affects finance, accounting, sales, marketing, and the web development team, pushing through change with your product becomes very hard. You absolutely need to understand how and why this existing process came to be before you can start selling your product. There may be several people whose entire job and paycheck relies on this dumb, stupid, illogical process.
- **How are purchasing decisions made?** Vital when selling to big companies, and vastly different than dealing with small companies. Do company managers have discretionary purchasing decisions at a certain level, or are purchases routed through finance. As an example, I've worked at a company where any technology-related purchases of $25,000

or greater required a 10-page questionnaire that was sent to the "Technology Processing Committee." From there, those approved would be sent to finance for review for available budget funds. If the funds were considered outside of the fiscal year's normal operating budget, the project was rejected or approved for the following fiscal year. But… if a purchase was $24,999, the individual product line manager and could gain approval from only their Vice President to move forward. So a local product manager could buy three products at $24,999 each, but could have a single purchase of $25,000 denied. This is selling to a big company.

- **Who is involved with these decisions?** There may not be a formal purchasing committee, but there is likely a team of people your target prospect consults for review and approval. Here's a great question: "Who do you bring into the conversation when evaluating products like ours?" Firstly, you enable the client to feel they are leading the process, instead of asking, "Who has to approve this purchase?" Secondly, you are fishing for information about whether or not a process is in place. If they say, "Oh, I always have Mike from Engineering and Sally from Sales look at everything…", you know the person you're speaking with has purchased products in the past. If they look at you blankly, you have some work to do in guiding the decision through their company.

- **Why is your product so interesting to them?** This question helps you reach the core reason why they really are interested.
  - o Pro Tip: It's not because your user interface is cool or because you have such-and-such feature. It's because they have a specific problem they think your product will solve. And that problem may have nothing to do with why you built the product in the first place.

- **At the end of your conversation, ask "What happens next?"** (see Michael Pedone at SalesBuzz). This gives you concrete action steps and commitment. If they say, "I'm not sure. Let me circulate your marketing materials and I'll get back to you…", then you're in trouble. Wrestle control back from the prospect with the suggestion to make recommendations and ask for permission to interview 2-3 other people at their company for their perspective on the target problem.

Be ready for a quick decision process, and then be ready to dig in for quite a long one (6-12 months) as the stakeholders at the target company get organized. There are rare occasions when you do meet the correct executive sponsor with budget, decision authority, and a migraine your product resolves. When this happens, a 6-12 month sales cycle may be compressed to 1-2 months. Key word: rarely.

What is the best way for a SaaS company to deal with long sales cycles when selling to the enterprise (i.e., business-to-business selling)?

(I'm assuming we are discussing an enterprise-wide SaaS platform or service that is priced at $25K-100K+ per year, or multiples of that, not single-user licenses that might range from $10-$100 per transaction.)

First and foremost, do NOT hire "closers." Instead, hire sales professionals that expect and thrive in complex organizational and major account selling. Any salesperson that prides himself on being a "closer" is the last person you want developing relationships with high-ticket customers. The Huthwaite Corporation studied over 35,000 sales calls and concluded that "closers" and closing techniques may have even a negative impact on enterprise-level sales.

In the enterprise sale, you're dealing with multiple decision-makers and committees (formal or informal). Your salesperson will be interacting with committee members numerous times over several months, and a cheap attempt to prematurely close the sale may cut off the sales process for your company altogether.

You cannot compress a six-month sales cycle into one-month just by hiring someone who claims to be "closer." Your clients are sophisticated managers who are seeking a solution for a difficult business problem. The sales process requires a sales professional to identify product champions, antagonists, and the critical business issues to target throughout the stages of the sale.

You will very rarely find a point in any conversation where your salesperson is even present to deliver a "closing line" (i.e., "It looks like you have all of information you need, so if you'll just sign here.... Use my pen.") Instead, the prospect's decision is an educational process in which your sales professional needs to be integrated in order to earn the sale. The contract and negotiation phase itself even after the decision is made will take several calls and offer opportunities for the sale to fail. (I also recommend "Trust-Based Selling"   -   http://www.amazon.com/Trust-Based-Selling-

Collaboration-Long-Term-Relationships/dp/0071461949.) In most big sales, the line is blurred between the decision, the contract execution, the initial payment, and an implementation phase which might last months or even a year.

Who do you want managing this process - a sales professional or a "closer" worried about delivering a cute line? Ultimately, of course, you want a sales professional that is comfortable with leading the prospect through the sales and contract process. This is not for the impatient "closer", but instead for a sales professional that genuinely cares about solving her client's problems.

Do not mistake "inside sales" with "telesales." Telesales are useful for the $100/month product or timeshares in Las Vegas. A true inside sales professional is a highly skilled individual that is able to develop relationships, read customer psychology, generate interaction effectively on a product demonstration, and motivate the prospect to take action, all over the phone.

If you're selling at the enterprise level, the initial point of contact is as critical as the initial sales presentation and approving the final contract. Who would you rather have at the point of contact with inbound conference lead or a Senior VP that just downloaded a white paper on your company's website after hearing about you in the Wall Street Journal, a technical sales expert or an inexperienced telesales person?

Use Targeted Marketing. Develop a series of touch points. Two to five page white papers offer your expertise and show your focus on solving the prospect's core business problems. Hosting a webinar event is a very inexpensive way to reach your market, and offers upstream/downstream market communication opportunities.

More Marketing Ideas:

- *Blog regularly.* This is an easy source of web traffic and shows your dedication to the industry. Even if the inbound web traffic fails, you can reuse the content for outbound marketing contact and to send to clients following a conversation as a means to add value to the sales conversation.

- ***Know your industry-specific news sites***. Use these articles as Twitter and LinkedIn Group posts, and send them to prospects after sales calls. It doesn't matter that you didn't create the content. It's your job to facilitate information and become an "idea hub" for your target clients.

- ***Offer to guest blog on industry news sites.*** Industry sites are constantly looking for content and opinions for their articles. This is free marketing and shows your expertise to the readership. I've done this for HousingWire for an industry conference. One article was retweeted 40+ times within a day of the event.

- ***Develop a regular outbound report or newsletter, and track open rates.*** There are plenty of inexpensive services (i.e. MailChimp and ConstantContact) that will help you identify leads and targets from your contact list.

I'm doing lots of demos and sending out proposals, but it seems like this is where my prospects are "going dark" and deals are stalling on me. What's going on?

It sounds like you are focusing on driving the sale to these points in the sales process that seem like big events, but are really nothing but a reason for the sales process to stall. It seems weird that once you've assessed the prospect's needs and showed your whiz-bang software or written up a proposal as requested, the opportunity would stall. If you measure the wrong events in the sales process, you'll end up getting what you measure.

Here are a few "Sales Vanity Metrics" to avoid in your sales process:

1. **Number of Outbound Calls**

   This means you are waiting for leads and prospects to call you back. And they don't. So instead, you tell yourself, "Sales is just a numbers game and if I make enough calls, I'll close some sales." This sounds an awful lot like the Infinite Monkey Theorem.

   Instead, measure number of leads converted to prospects or number of sales advances from your outbound calls. Making 10 calls and logging five advances is far better than making 45 outbound calls with no progress on your sales opportunities.

2. **Number of Product Demos**

   Demos stall the sale, because you think the product is the reason the prospect is interested. Measuring the number of demos causes you to rush to the demo before properly assessing the client's situation and the problem they need to solve.

   It's not your product; it's how you can to solve the prospect's problem. In fact, see how far you can take a sale without showing your product. And when you need to, see how short you can keep your demo.

Check out "Great Demo!" for more on this at www.seconderivative.com.

3. Number of Free Trials

If you are measuring the number of free trials, what you're really doing is sending logins and pass codes to accounts will never be used. It sounds good, because you think the person is really interested, so much so that they want to use your product. For free. Without any commitment. And they can screen your phone calls, never login, and never talk to you again. Yeah, that sounds great doesn't it?

Instead of "free trials," call them "Problem Assessments" where you and the prospect mutually agree on how the new user account will be applied to a specific problem the prospect is facing. Set a deadline and then assess whether your product solved their problem. (Hint: Set up the rules to the game so you win.)

Here's a nice article on Cohort Analysis (http://chrislema.com/are-you-doing-cohort-analysis/) for your free trial, er Problem Assessments.

4. Number of Proposals

After your demo, your prospect says, "This looks great. Send me a proposal." You fist pump because you get to notch BOTH a demo and a proposal on your Sales Vanity Metrics.

Proposals are nothing but a reason to stall. A typical proposal includes a product description, price, delivery, training, implementation, and contract length. When you send a proposal, you're giving the prospect a list of reasons to reject your product – "not the right product", "too expensive", "not a good time", "need more training", etc., etc., etc.

Instead of proposals, write out a Project Implementation Plan with the client. Ask them what should be included so that the project is approved internally. Make them put in just as much work as you, so you have a clear picture of what they exactly need.

Read more about "Vanity Metrics" for Startups here:

http://www.startuplessonslearned.com/2009/12/why-vanity-metrics-are-dangerous.html.

Proposals, Pricing & Contracts

What is the best way for shifting the discussion when they seem to really want a proposal? Some of our leads want proposals, but those convert badly, even when they say they really like the proposal.

It is particularly problematic when they are looking at multiple vendors and we don't know what consideration will end up making the decision for them. This compounds with how challenging good estimates are; if we play it safe we come in too high, but if we don't then we mismanage expectations and cause problems for the project later.

What is the best way for shifting the discussion when they seem to really want a proposal? We have pretty proposals now. Is there any way that can be used well as a sales tool? I'd rather never have to put another one together, but if it will help close a big deal....

Ask yourself: "who has control of the sale?" Once you send the proposal, you've ceded control of the sale to the prospect. That's bad. In a "Lean Startup" sense, the number of proposals sent are a vanity metric (as are the number of demos given).

> *Tip: see http://www.startuplessonslearned.com/2009/12/why-vanity-metrics-are-dangerous.html by Eric Ries for more about "vanity metrics" for your startup.*

When a prospect asks - "Can you send me a proposal?" You can counter with a few options:

1. **"Sure, tell me everything that should be in it in order for us to go ahead and get started with you."**

   This is a bit aggressive, but very clear you expect the proposal will be mutually developed and lead to approval, not a document they will muse over.

2. **"Sure, to do that, let's talk through a few more details of the project. For example, we've talked about 2-3 options of what you have in mind for a final site design. Let's nail that down now."**

   or

   "Sure thing. I think we have most of what we need. We haven't talked in detail about the project economics and delivery timeline. Tell more about these so I can be sure to include what you're thinking in our work plan."

   > This approach helps you smoke out objections. If they aren't willing to talk about final design or budget or timeline, then you don't have a real prospect (or decision-maker). They might even say - "Jeez, I'm not sure on the budget..." to which you reply - "Great! So, who do we talk with to walk through options?"

3. **"Sure thing. We write up 'Work Plans' all the time for clients. This is the framework around the project as we both expect it to run."**

   Then, go through the each part of what would be in a proposal and have them help you write it.

Notice each response begins with an affirmative. You want the client to think they are in control by agreeing to their idea of a "proposal", but you direct the conversation in a way in which you maintain control. You can also say, "Sure - that's a great idea!..."

A proposal in a traditional sense is nothing more than a tailored brochure for that prospect with pricing. If you don't have every detail outlined and an agreement on price, the probability of you preparing a proposal to 100% match the prospect's expectations are almost nil.

"Send me a proposal" is also a signal you are not talking with the final decision-maker. Whoever is asking for the proposal wants to review it and present it themselves. When I think about a final decision-maker, it's rare that I can imagine her sitting down and reviewing a 20-page proposal page by page in order to make a decision.

Instead, just like with business plans, decision-makers read the executive summary and make decisions by talking with entrepreneurs. The same goes when you are selling complex services.

As for the pretty proposal document, use it as the work plan if it is functionally designed. If not, than scrap it, except in extreme cases where it's proposal or nothing with the client. And if that's the case, do you really want to work with such a client? Government contracts do require proposals, but you don't gain points in their evaluation criteria for aesthetics.

What are best practices related to auto-renewal of SaaS/enterprise software contracts?

1. **Start with a 90-day notice required for termination and be ready to agree to a 30-day notice.** You can use this as a bargaining chip during negotiation. It doesn't really matter to you if it's 30, 60, or 90 days. A cancel is a cancel and having two months extra notice isn't going to help the revenue pain much. Besides, do you really have the ligation firepower to challenge the client who cancelled with only 79 days notice instead of 90?

   Expect that customers will break this cancellation clause anyway. I'm sure the people you're dealing with in selling your service are very nice and don't expect to break this clause, but if you sign a contract in April and your customer is told by their management to cut Q4 costs in September, you might be out of luck either way.

2. If your customers are balking at any type of auto-renew, **offer your new client a 90-day "out clause"**, meaning you'll give them 90 days at the start of the contract to cancel without harm. This shows good faith on your end, plus motivates the buyer to implement your solution quickly. If your product is as good as you say it is, no one will exercise this clause but you'll be viewed very positively for including it.

3. **Use the auto-renew as a chip for "price protection."** If you client balks at the auto-renew, tell them:

   "We include this to provide you with protection against price resets. As we continue to build functionality over time, we expect we will charge 50% or even 100% more for our product a year from now. By including this auto-renew clause, it retains the pricing we've agreed to now."

4. But... If you use the "price protection" concept, also **add a clause that allows you to reset the price to a higher level after three (3) years**, but not lower. For example, if you are charging $5000/month now and your customer continues to auto-renew, by year 3, you might be charging the market $10,000/month. Be sure you have the ability to reset the price

at a higher level. You can include a discount from the future market price, such as "the rest prices after three (3) years will be equal to 75% of the price for services paid by any client of [INSERT YOUR COMPANY]."

5. **Insert language that includes some sort of penalty for early termination.** Something to the equivalent of 1-3 months of subscription fees paid as a lump sum is fair.

6. **Be prepared for companies to require the omission or deletion of the auto-renew clause.** Some companies have internal policies against this because it saves them from lost contracts signed by "so-so who was crazy and left the company." Four years later, the contract surfaces and suddenly someone in legal during a contract audit realizes they've been paying for a service no one uses. If that's the case, be ready to request some other concession. That might be a higher upfront payment or a cancellation payment.

Send auto-renew notices to your clients after the new period is initiated. It's tempting to let sleeping dogs lie, but it will ultimately be to your benefit to be transparent to your clients and their legal team. More so, you should be communicating with your clients regularly anyway, so that the conversation around service renewal is brief and expected.

What are some ways a salesperson can speed along the procurement process when dealing with large Fortune 1,000 companies?

We're seeing major lag times with large customers from the time we have a "handshake" agreement to the time when our deals actually get through a large company's procurement process. We've stripped down our MSA/SOW document, but find most large companies prefer to use their own document. Our changes tend to be fairly minor. However, we're seeing that the back-n-forth can take 3+ months or more in some cases. Is there anything we can do to help speed things along? I'd love to get some answers from people who work in procurement.

The big issue is it seems like procurement in large companies is a bit of a black hole. The buyer doesn't seem to know how to navigate their own procurement team or how long it will likely take.

1. **Make sure you are selling to the correct person.**

   If a senior manager is bought into your solution, there should be no delays. Take the extreme case: If Tim Cook at Apple decided he wanted to use a new vendor for iPhone production, do you think it would take a long time to have Apple's procurement team approve the decision?

   If you are finding the procurement process is taking longer than expected, it may mean your buyer is a lower-ranking manager that hasn't purchased frequently (if at all) from vendors and they don't know the fast track to approvals.

   Your prospect may be using "procurement" as an excuse to gaining approval from her manager for budget, while purposely withholding this information from you and now they're too embarrassed to tell you otherwise.

2. **Take control of the procurement process**
   Ask for the names and contact info (email AND phone) for the legal, accounting, and vendor management personnel from your prospective client, once you reach the "handshake" milestone. This prevents the additional layer of

communication from you to your buyer to the internal team, then...

3. **Host a "Procurement Kick-off" conference call with your prospect and their legal rep, accounts payable manager, and vendor manager.**

Position this call to your buyer like this:

> "I'm sure your legal and procurement team will have questions of our legal/procurement people. To expedite that, let's have a 15-minute conference call between you and your team and me for an introduction."

During this call, ask these questions about their process:

- *"What is the normal turnaround time for this sort of process?"* This will help you manage your expectations. Sometimes, it simply takes 3-4 months from your buyer. That's just the way they do business.
- *"What are the 2-3 stumbling blocks that slow the approval process when you are setting up new vendors?"* This will provide you with land mines to avoid. Procurement managers LOVE this question. They appreciate that you understand their work and that you want to make life easy for them. You'd be surprised at how something small makes a big difference here. For example, while you may hate sending email attachments and prefer to link to your document on Google Drive, the procurement office may use project tracking software that stores contract versions automatically when sent via email. When you send the link to Google Drive, the procurement manager has to download it, save it and then upload it manually into this system without the reference to the email discussing this specific version. Yes, really.
- *"Do you have a Master Vendor Agreement that you would prefer we use instead of me sending our SOW?"* Chances are your prospect has spent many hours and lots of dollars protecting themselves

and the odds your home-grown SOW matches up with their requirements is pretty small. Start with their template to avoid over-zealous red-lining of your document by their team. You can always add Appendices and Exhibits to their Master Agreement to include key information from your SOW.

Schedule an update phone conference once a week or every two weeks at the onset of the procurement process. Tell your prospect, "I know this is important for both of us, so setting up these short conference calls will help us all stay on point."

Write a summary email of action steps and expected completion dates at the onset of the procurement process and use this as a working document during your scheduled conference calls.

- Use Bullet Points
- Think of the action steps
- Like a list of to-dos
- This makes life easier for both sides

Remember, the procurement team has performance ratings as well. If they take a long time to approve new vendors to the frustration of business managers, this will hurt them personally over the long run. When you show a vested interest in helping them expedite an agreement, they will appreciate it.

4. **PICK UP THE PHONE** (yes, caps intentional!)

Once you are in a back-and-forth banter with the prospect's legal team on changes and red-lining, whenever you receive an inbound email with suggested changes, PICK UP THE PHONE and call the person immediately to clarify.

If you fall into the email trap, by the time you type a response and send it, your counter-party might be gone for the day or on to the next project. You are probably 1 of 20 projects for that person. When they send the email, you know they're thinking about you - everything is fresh in their mind.

(Not to mention the personal relationship you'll develop by actually talking with someone compared to email...)

5. **Consider providing your service to your client in parallel to the formal approval.**

   This might include account set up, training, and other assistance that will achieve lock in and thus provide an incentive for your prospect to push the approvals through.

   BE CAREFUL though - set a date by which you will suspend service if the procurement process is not completed. If it is agreed during your "Procurement Kick-off" meeting that you will have the executed contract and initial payment completed by a certain date, set this as your suspension date and put this in an email and continue to mention it during your "Procurement Update" meetings.

6. **Begin the "Business Sale" during the "Technical Sale."**

   This concept is described by Brian Burns in "Selling in a New Market Space" (www.amazon.com/Selling-New-Market-Space-Innovative/dp/0071636102). If you are advancing the "Technical Sale" with your prospect, then propose that you initiate the contract process to help to accelerate the approval once a final decision is made.

Be careful how you use this; avoid it too early in the process, or else it will make it appear you are attempting an "assumptive close" with your prospect. Use your intuition. Perhaps you've completed a second product demo to your prospect and her team, and now she's giving you signals that senior management is ready to approve this purchase. At this point, suggest that while she is scheduling time with senior management to present (which may take WEEKS because of schedules), you would like to have a preliminary call with your prospect's procurement team to have them preview your Statement of Work for any show-stoppers or suggested language changes they know will be required.

Software-as-a-Service (SaaS): Is it a good idea to offer a discount for the launch of a Saas B2B service?

Companies still do launches?

I assume you've gone through the Customer Discovery and Customer Development process, which means you have hard data to support pricing expectations, because you already have users paying for "Minimal Viable Product" (in Lean Startup vernacular).

Customer Development Model

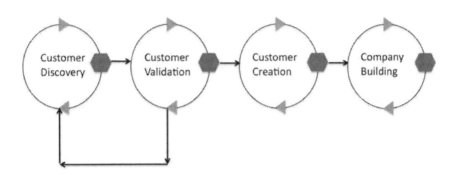

If you're launching blind, save your resources and retreat back to Customer Development activity. During Customer Development, begin at your planned discounted price (or lower) for the first few customers and then migrate your ask price upwards with each new customer you board with your pre-launch version. When price becomes a real issue in advancing the sale or it appears a higher price requires additional executive approvals at your target companies that extend the sales timeline, you know you've hit your limit. Of course, you may choose to deal with the additional decision layers and longer timelines. It's just a matter of time-to-close rates, metrics you also need to measure and optimize for your business.

Whether you strictly follow The Lean Startup™ Methodology or not, you absolutely must validate your market, product, and price before a big launch.

Do not mistake price as a real objection. Price is never the reason for purchasing or not purchasing. Price is a benchmark for customer perceived value. If a customer balks at price, they are telling you that you have not yet conveyed the perceived value necessary to justify the expenditure. The price-to-value metric varies from industry to industry, and from individual to individual. This is a primary discovery you must make in your Customer Discovery and Customer Development phases.

But if you must offer a discount...

Explain clearly to your customers this is "Launch Pricing." Additionally, explain the initial pricing is only available for the first year (or first six months). Document this into your user agreement, so there are no questions at renewal for both your local users and their vendor managers. I've personally found myself in situations where a verbal agreement was made with software users and local managers, but at renewal time, the vendor manager based renewal pricing solely on past pricing. Worse, vendor managers may be evaluated based on discounts negotiated with vendors. In the case of Launch Pricing, you'll be fighting just to retain current pricing at renewal, let alone pushing the price up to "List Price."

Rest assured you will receive pushback at renewal time regardless. The client may either request an extension of your Launch Pricing, or seek other concessions such as upgraded service, additional service and training beyond your normal standards, or additional seat licenses.

It's likely you will introduce new features and functionality throughout the product's life, so log these features to have an account of how much the product is enhanced between Launch Pricing and renewal, supporting the move to List Price.

Ask for something in return for the price discount. Software is a non-rivalrous good - you cannot pull the "I've got another person coming by this afternoon who's also interested in this car, and it's the last on the lot like it" trick, so you need to create scarcity and conditions another way.

- Create a "New Subscribers Cohort." Explain to customers that in order to properly support customers at this price, you are going to bring them through implementation and training as a class. Limit your New Subscriber Cohort to 5 or 10 companies, thus creating scarcity for your non-rivalrous good at Launch Pricing.
- Host monthly calls. In return for the Launch Pricing, require monthly calls to ask about client satisfaction, feature ideas, and cases studies.
- Get video and written testimonials after three months.
- Require two hours of work at your next trade show booth. Ask for them to work at a trade show exhibit, so you have a live testimonial for booth traffic.
- Use of their names and quotes in your launch press release.

You should consider these ideas for all new customers at special or regular pricing, but particularly at Launch Pricing, so there is a cost to the customer in exchange for a lower price. **You may find some customers appreciate these obligations, but will instead pay you full price to avoid them.**

Prepare to deal with companies that choose not to buy at launch. They may simply want to see how the product does before jumping in or they have internal purchasing barriers at the time of your launch, such as budget constraints or recent executive leadership changes hindering major purchasing decisions. When they are ready to buy, they may well ask or even require that you honor your Launch Pricing, especially if they were in your sales pipeline during launch. You'll then either need to honor that price with the client obligations (or without) or risk a shaky start to the relationship.

While your Launch Price objective is to create perceived value for those customers that take advantage of your Launch Pricing, instead you could be anchoring the market to your lower price instead.[11]

---

[11] Read more about Anchoring Effects here: http://en.wikipedia.org/wiki/Anchoring.

Now, ask yourself if it's really worth the cost to discount your price at launch.

Sales & Email Marketing

What are the basics of marketing a B2B product online?

Find your voice. Think pull, THEN push. Get personal when you can. Start and participate in Meetup Groups. Be a leader within the group by organizing individual events and providing value. There are seemingly hundreds of apps in the B2B world that each are allegedly designed to increase revenues, reduce costs, and increase efficiency. If you don't break through the noise, you won't be noticed.

Attract target prospects to your site by contributing to your industry's conversation and showing your expertise. Then, you'll find your inbound leads will be much more qualified and the starting relationship much stronger. Once you have these relationships formed, add value with regular communication and personal attention.

With the number of outlets available, find the 3-4 best communication channels where your target audience is spending their time, then pound away at these places as a thought leader and contributor.

For a B2B product, these will be different for each product and industry. A few general places might include:

- **LinkedIn**. Find select groups and contribute to the conversation. Do not sell on these groups and avoid groups that are spammy (you'll know them when you see them). Posts to LinkedIn groups should be relevant news articles (use Google News alerts to push these to you every day) and links to solid resources, such as white papers and webcasts, and conference presentations.

- **Quora**. This is a fabulous place to meet prospective clients. Ever been on a Quora date? Find out who is "up" voting answers and follow key questions relevant to your industry. People on Quora are here because they want to know more things. Use that to your advantage.

- **Twitter**. Engage without expecting a direct lead. Lots of perspectives on Twitter for B2B. My approach is to share content and articles, have some back-and-forth with others in the industry, and point the community to excellent resources. If all you're doing on Twitter is posting links to your blog or product, you'll get tuned out. Don't puke on everyone.

- **Webcasts, e-books, and white papers.** These are easy to post and repurpose. Host the webcast even if no one shows up, record it and reuse the content on your blog or send the recording to prospects.

What are best practices for sending "cold" sales emails?

The specific use case is SaaS sales but could be related to any sales process. There has been a lot written about cold calling, but much less about "cold emailing". What are the best practices?

Don't send cold emails intended for sales purposes.

Do:
1. Pick up the phone
2. Find the decision maker
3. Network your way to an introduction
4. Start lower in the organization and work your way up
5. Leave the emails to marketing

Unless...
1. Your email is customized for each prospect and is part of an outreach plan. And even then, use sparingly. It is very, very easy for a target prospect to hit "reply" with "not interested."
2. Your email is intended to locate a decision-maker (per Aaron Ross's method described in "Predictable Revenue").

I recently watched a webinar hosted by Bryan Kreuzberger at BreakthroughEmail (www.breakthroughemail.com). Check out their website, where you can register and download a nifty guide to sending cold emails.

You absolutely need to create your own emails and test response rates for YOUR product and YOUR market and YOUR target buyers. Find resources like these and read them, and then test, test, test.

Most importantly, remember it is called "email marketing," NOT "email selling." Do not try to sell your product via email. Use email as a communication medium to set the next action – set an appointment, request information, confirmation an appointment, or send an agenda. If you're pitching in your email, then stop.

What are good ways to say no to prospects when they are interested but want to have case studies from you before moving forward?

I hear quite often from prospects, "your solution is interesting, but help me with case studies etc. so I can generate traction internally why it makes sense for us to introduce your solution on our platform". How do I avoid this? I don't have time to educate clients like this. Are they too lazy to recognize business opportunities and/or additional revenue by themselves?

You are correct – you don't have time to educate clients like this. Your time should be spent learning, not educating. You need to learn about client issues, business problems, and the history of how they have attempted to solve this problem so far. Case studies can be effective for branding and marketing, and as a startup you don't care about such things. You care about boarding a new client.

"I hear quite often…" means you're asking clients to figure out how they should use your product. This could mean you are rushing to product demos too quickly without assessing the prospect's need.

"I hear quite often…" is telling you that you haven't helped this person identify a critical business issue, and how your product will solve this problem.

Double-back and start the sales process over with situational analysis and needs analysis. Once you uncover a critical business issue, your prospect won't care if they're the only ones in the world using your product.

I read a story about a salesperson who used case studies from an airline company they served at a manufacturing company. The salesperson thought because both companies were large, it would be useful to the prospect. The prospect stood up, walked over to the window and then said to the salesperson, "That's funny. I don't think we have any airplanes here…"

What are the most effective direct marketing strategies for a SaaS product?

Live by the mantra: "Add value, add value, add value." Provide new perspectives on an industry challenge or problem. If you're a new entrant to the industry (e.g., an engineer tackling human resources compliance software systems), that's all the more opportunity you have to be unique in your approach.

White papers

- Keep these short and sweet, 3-5 pages max. Add a few pretty graphs to help with readability. (Hey, that's just the way it works.)
- Post to your website for lead generation ("Fill out the form to download...").
- For online lead gen, provide a clear synopsis of the paper. Don't shroud the paper's topic in hopes that curiosity will increase lead gen.
- Never pitch your product in your white paper. Be a thought leader. Save the selling for your sales calls.

Webcasts

- Record and then post to your blog/website. Don't tell people before the webcast or at the beginning you are recording. It will decrease registrations and people will tune out thinking they'll go back at watch later.
- Slice up the recording into small segments and use for expanded blog posts on each concept.
- Put a short segment on your site and use a lead form to convert the visitor to view the entire recording.
- Keep these to 30 minutes. Start on time and end on time. Twenty minutes of content and 10 minutes of Q&A. Have some prepared questions from the audience in case you don't get any interaction when you ask for questions at the end, so you're not sitting there saying, "Really? No questions?"

- Jump into the concept quickly. I registered for a 25-minute webinar last week and the presenter spent the first five minutes talking about their company and product. Don't do this.

Guest articles, Blog posts & Podcast

- There are plenty of industry publications, big and small, looking for content.
- Post short articles to your own blog and then proactively send these out to your contact list weekly. You need not sit and wait for visitors or blog subscribers.
- If you're uncomfortable sending out a blanket email with blog posts, use the posts with individual leads and personalize the email, "I saw your presentation at Dreamforce last month and thought you'd appreciate my point of view on the issue of social media and enterprise sales..."

Write an eBook

I've done this myself. This book case in point, and "Startup Selling: How to sell if you really, really have to and don't know how" at http://www.amazon.com/Startup-Selling-sell-really-Volume/dp/1468159240. I give away copies to startup founders at various events and to attendees of my workshops. I went the more standard ebook route by writing, editing, and publishing a "book" as compared to the Hubspot approach. I used Create Space for my set up and distribution. It's incredible how differently you are received by people when they learn you've written a book.

- See: "Self-Publishing Your Own Book is the New Business Card" at http://www.jamesaltucher.com/2012/01/self-publishing-your-own-book-is-the-new-business-card.
- Check out HubSpot and their approach on Marketing Whitepapers & Ebooks: http://www.hubspot.com/internet-marketing-whitepapers. I see Hubspot on Twitter constantly promoting their free ebooks and guides. They are primarily glorified PowerPoint decks, but the "book" grabs people's attention.

- See: "Three Mac apps to help you self publish your book" at http://gigaom.com/2012/11/10/three-mac-apps-to-help-you-self-publish-your-book.

A recent Harvard Business Review article describes insight selling ("The End of Solution Sales" at http://hbr.org/2012/07/the-end-of-solution-sales). These principles apply to SaaS product marketing. Whether a SaaS product intermediates a manual process or replaces an existing technology, the product is usually fighting status quo ("we know it's not perfect but it works for us..."). You need to provide new insights and perspectives. Be creative. Really creative. The OkCupid blog is a great example of using data to approach the online dating industry (See: 10 Charts About Sex" at http://blog.okcupid.com/index.php/10-charts-about-sex).

Sales Tools & Technology

What are some ways technology is changing the job of a salesperson?

For the worse:

1. **Fewer phone calls.** Reps are too dependent on email. For early stage prospecting, fire off emails to new leads to request a time to call or they reply to a lead form submission with an email instead of picking up the phone to talk to them. Later in the process, reps continue emails with 20+ "Re:" in the string for simple communication like confirming the time and place of the next meeting, or for more complex communication, such as handling objections.

   If the sales reps were required to use the phone, they would call directly to uncover the root cause of product questions, the "why?" behind the "what?" question.

2. **Less preparedness for sales calls.** With CRMs, reps are pulling up account and contact notes as they are dialing the phone, thinking they can refresh themselves on an account as the prospect's phone is ringing.

   Before CRM software, reps had notebooks or notecards they would lay out to link together a clear understanding of where they stood in the sales process and what they needed to accomplish in their next call.

3. **Too much dependence on product demos.** With screen-sharing software, jumping into a demo is far too easy. Reps are depending on the product to sell instead of performing fundamental needs assessment and proposing client solutions based on those needs. Before technology, leading a product demo generally meant an on-site meeting, an expensive activity because of the time investment and travel expense. Therefore, the demo took place far later in the sales process.

   Related to this, reps also fire off PowerPoint decks and product sheets instead of retaining that information for on-site conversations.

For the better:

1. **Opportunity tracking.** CRMs provide a much clearer picture of how long an opportunity has been live and its stage in the sales process. This enables managers to hold reps more accountable for daily and weekly activity.
2. **More meetings.** While reps make fewer calls, the screen-sharing applications do enable reps to pull together more decision-makers and influencers because they can meet any time during the day or week the prospect and her team is available, instead of planning around plane schedules and weather.
3. **More contact with clients.** iPhones > Pay phones. While seemingly growing larger with each version, I'll take a smartphone over a bag of quarters and an address book any day.

What are the best tools you use in terms of ROI when you want to increase your sales?

Think of ROI as Customer Acquisition Costs (CAC). A good CRM enables you to track this. More importantly, think through what you need to effectively track ROI/CAC.

1. **Log your travel time and costs *(if you are traveling)* and calculate your "Cost per call" and "Cost per meeting."**

   Start by tracking your weekly outbound call rates, conversion rates, and average revenue per user (ARPU) when you are calling from your office. This should be considered as an opportunity cost as part of your CACs. You might find your ultimate sales ROI is lower when you travel because of the time and money spent to get face-to-face with the prospect.

   Also, log when in the sales process you are getting face-to-face with clients. You might find ways to determine more efficiencies there. Maybe you are traveling too soon in the process, yielding a smaller ROI for that expense or that by traveling too soon in the process, you are putting yourself in a position in which the client expects a second (or third or fourth!) face-to-face meeting before they sign the contract.

2. **Determine the flow of lead generation (sources) and their intrinsic costs - AdWords vs. conferences vs. old fashioned research.**

   Log these leads into a CRM such as Salesforce. This can be automated for web leads and entered manually for other leads, such as referrals, inbound calls, and conference leads. Be specific and be consistent. For referrals, write the exact person "Joe Smith", not just "friend." For conference leads, write out the conference, month/year, and day - "Dreamforce 9/12 Day 1." This will enable you to run reports on these leads for conversion rate, average revenue per user (ARPU), and time to close. By including the year, you can assess your year-over-year performance. Maybe you'll discover conference leads take longer to close and have a lower ARPU, but have a significantly higher conversion rate. Maybe referrals close quickly with higher ARPUs but the conversion rates are lower. It sure would be interesting to know if none of your Day 3 leads at Dreamforce closed but 15% of your Day 1 leads did.

3. **Overlay these tracking systems with Marketing Initiatives** (e.g., start of Google AdWords campaign, conference booth expenditure, outbound email campaign to previous website registrants). Plug-ins are available for most major CRMs, such as MailChimp for SalesForce to make this tracking faster and more accurate.

Startups: What is the best use of snail mail for SaaS startups?

Reasons I've used snail mail:

1. **For "Thank you" cards** following a significant conversation or meeting. I've used these and am always surprised how surprised the recipients are to receive a handwritten note from me.

2. **For "Thank you" cards to conference organizers and speakers.** Even if you haven't personally met the individual to whom you're sending, conference organizers are seemingly always under-appreciated for the work they do. For many speakers, it is a privilege to speak at a conference and many spend lots of long, hard hours preparing remarks or their panel presentations. Sending a genuine note of thanks with a specific point or two you learned from their presentation.

3. **To send copies of a book I've written** as a thank you gift or to ask for the person's review. Do the same with a white paper, with a request to bring it along with them for their morning commute or next plane trip during take-off and landing when electronic devices are prohibited.

4. **To send a copy of a book you may have mentioned or suggested in a sales conversation**. This is super simple on Amazon to have it shipped directly.

5. **To send photographs,** especially if the person was a speaker or featured in some way at an event. Everyone snaps photos on their phone, but no one prints them out anymore. You could also snap a picture of your team and have everyone sign it as a promissory note for great service, or just after signing up a new customer.

6. **To send hard copies of scholarly journal articles.** Many scholarly journals require an expensive subscription to read articles on line. If you have access to one, or if you can swing by a local university library to make copies, this is a pretty cool way to differentiate yourself. I have access to JSTOR b/c of some adjunct teaching I do, so this is easier for me - I can just download and print/email. Use Google Scholar (http://scholar.google.com) to locate academic journal

articles. Many times there are PDFs available for download without a fee.

What are the must-have business development apps for 2013?

A telephone.

Selling only happens in conversations with your prospects where you can assess needs, ask questions, ask for clarity, and watch responses to questions and ideas.

I tell clients over and over and over to PICK UP THE PHONE. (Yes, caps intentional!) Email should only be used for communication between phone calls to set up times and send agendas. Email is NOT a selling tool. CRMs are not selling tools. Email marketing software is NOT a selling tool. They help you organize your leads and prospects. They do not help you sell.

Besides, if you call and get voicemail, you can give yourself permission to call back at a later day or time, and you can notify the person that you are sending an email. This draws their attention to an email that otherwise might be ignored.

Example 1: The Contract

The phone saves time on projects. What if you are negotiating a contract and you receive a long list of questions from the contracting manager of your soon-to-be client? It's Thursday morning, just before lunch. Crafting and drafting an email response to her 12 questions will take you the afternoon and you hit send around 4:30 pm. Except... Oops... you receive an out-of-office message that she's now on vacation through the end of next week and will return your email as quickly as possible.

Huh?

Had you picked up the phone immediately when you received the email, you would have likely caught the contract manager right away and could have discussed her questions right then. Instead, you're stuck waiting for more than 10 days, unless you can find someone else at your target prospect to help you.

Example 2: A New Lead

You receive notice of new registration on your website. While providing a phone number is optional on your registration form, the new lead enters it anyway. Instead of calling, you decide to send an email reply to their registration, asking how they found your website and how you can help them.

And then you wait. And wait. And wait. And a few days later, you finally remember you never got a reply to your email. What now? Had you picked up the phone and called right away, you could have qualified the lead and shown a proclivity for quick response times.

Example 3: Post-Demo

You just finished a product demo with your product champion and three of his colleagues. The call wraps up with your Product Champion telling you he'll get with the team and get back to you. So you send a follow up email thanking him for his time and look forward to hearing back.

And you wait. And then you wait. And wait. And wait. And a few days later, you wait some more. And he never gets back to you.

Instead, you could have called your Product Champion immediately after the call and asked for his feedback and what next steps you should take.

What are good books and resources to read to become better at business development?

1. <u>Macro Process</u>: Strategy and process with a multi-step sales process
    - **The Huthwaite Institute & Neil Rackham** - Developed "SPIN Selling" and "Major Account Sales Strategy" (www.huthwaite.com). These books are bibles when it comes to the enterprise sale.
    - **Brian Burns** - "Selling in a New Market" (http://www.amazon.com/Selling-New-Market-Space-Innovative/dp/0071636102).
    - **Robert Miller & Stephen Heiman** - "The New Strategic Selling" (http://www.amazon.com/New-Strategic-Selling-Successful-Companies/dp/044669519X).
    - **Geoffrey Moore** - "Crossing the Chasm" (http://www.amazon.com/Crossing-Chasm-Marketing-Disruptive-Mainstream/dp/0060517123).
2. <u>Micro Process</u>: Why people buy, personal branding, conversations, sales process
    - **Jeffrey Gitomer** - (www.gitomer.com).
    - **Dale Carnegie** - "How to Win Friends and Influence People" (http://www.amazon.com/How-Win-Friends-Influence-People/dp/0671027034).
    - **Aaron Ross** - "Predictable Revenue" (www.predictablerevenue.com). This is an outstanding playbook to use for building your sales development and account management team. Very detailed with excellent examples and descriptions.
    - **Scott Sambucci** – "Startup Sales: How to sell if you really, really have to and don't know how." (http://www.amazon.com/Startup-Selling-sell-really-Volume/dp/1468159240) I wrote this and the reviews are very positive. I wrote this book with the startup entrepreneur in mind, discussing the key areas of establishing an enterprise sales process. It covers everything from sales calls to prospecting to conferences to the sales process.

3. **Tactical**: Phone strategies, leaving voicemails, asking the right questions, effective demonstrations

- **Michael Pedone** (www.salesbuzz.com/).
- **Brian Tracy** - "The Psychology of Selling" (Audio - http://briantracy.com/catalog/psychology-of-selling-plus-bonuses).
- **Peter Cohan** - "GreatDemo!" (www.secondderivative.com/).

How can I find upsell and cross-sell opportunities with my clients?

Schedule regular meetings (monthly, quarterly, or annually depending on your product and industry) specifically to discuss strategic changes to your client's business. Ask, "What's changed or do you see changing in your business in the next 3, 6, 12 months?" Just listen. Don't sell or pitch products. Take notes and come back to the client with specific ideas based on what you learned. If your clients ask about specific products, tell them you would love to talk about them in detail next week when you are prepared to discuss them with more preparation. This is so very professional and also quietly moves you into a sales process for that product, without the rigidity of calling to set an appointment about it.

Treat these meetings as you would an information-gathering sales call with a new lead or prospect. You wouldn't try to sell on the first call with a new prospect, so don't do it here.

An advantage to this approach is that if your customer has changes coming down the road, and you have a product in development or beta stage, it's an opportunity for you to get your product team involved with an existing customer as an early adopter or beta tester. The client benefits here because they are first to market. You benefit because, assuming you have a solid relationship, if the new product fails in some way, there is less pressure on you and your company.

Additionally, you can also influence the strategic direction of your client by educating them on new products and services you have in development. Many times, the client has an idea or vision, but execution of that vision requires something that either doesn't exist or isn't available. That presents an opportunity for you to define criteria for the purchase around the specs for your products in the development pipeline and blocking out your competition before an opportunity or RFP becomes public.

What is the best way of recording sales calls for sales management review?

If you're subscribed to GoToMeeting or WebEx, you can record calls using their application. Each GoToMeeting sets up a conference call number and the screen sharing. You need not use the screen sharing to record a call. However, you do need to remember to press the "Record" button when you start the call.

More recently, I've started using WebEx. When you are setting up the call in WebEx, there is an option to "Automatically Record This Call." This helps you avoid the need to remember to record. WebEx stores the recording and you can share the recordings simply by sending a URL link generated for each call. The recipient of the link need not be subscribed, nor do they need to login to listen or view the file. GoToMeeting requires you to store the recorded file on your own drive.

There are probably other good options; these are the two I've used. For general screen sharing without recording, check out Join.me. This is a free service, but does not record calls. This is my backup for all calls if, for whatever reason, the other caller is not able to open or download the WebEx software client. This happens on occasion because of individual computer settings or firewalls, but very rarely.

I have our sales team record calls regularly and go back and critique their own calls looking specifically for three aspects of the call that went well and three places to improve next time around.

What are some ways for a non-US Software-as-a-Service (SaaS) company with proprietary technology to reach people and potential clients for their business? We are a B2B company only, selling our product only to other enterprises.

I suggest hosting regular webcasts and webinars, tackling key topics in your industry. This highlights your expertise in the area and will attract people that are more likely to make a switch to product that is discernibly better than their status quo, because they are looking for information and resources outside of their current solution.

You can record these and repost them to a company blog or transcribe them and work into a white paper. Use the recording or white paper as outbound marketing content after the webcast. If no one shows, run the webcast anyway and pretend there are people there. When it's time for questions, just pretend someone did ask a question by saying, "Here's a question that is often asked..." This way you're not suggesting a specific question someone asked, though recording listeners might think this. Use this trick even if there are only two or three attendees.

Frequently cases like this are instructed to invest in search engine optimization (SE0). I disagree with this approach at the start for three (3) reasons:

1. It's likely to be too expensive a position for a bootstrapped company. And besides...
2. Investing in SEO can be fruitless. I am familiar enough with the SEO industry to know there are many, many, many "SEO Experts" out there. How can you possibly know which of these "experts" is the right fit for your company? This is throwing money into a black hole, and ...
3. You probably don't know what keywords and search terms are best at converting clear opportunities and revenue yet. First, generate organic traffic via blog posts and other content to learn what search terms are bringing traffic to you. Then, determine the conversion rates for these. It makes no sense

to drive traffic from search engines if the keywords used aren't converting. Said otherwise, would you rather have 100 visitors with no business or 10 visitors with three of these visitors converting to customers?

Focus on content development as part of your daily practice, with the rest of your time spent selling not marketing. You can scream at the top of your lungs with marketing, but until you are talking one-on-one with your target customer, you won't know what message matters to them.

Once you learn what effective traffic is converting, then you can focus on optimizing your site and using Google AdWords. Check out the Google Keyword Tool: https://adwords.google.com/o/KeywordTool. This is an excellent tool for identifying "long tail" search words. You might be surprised how some search terms generate thousands of keywords that exactly match your business, yet have very little competition, making the Google AdWords investment far more palatable.

As a startup, focus on direct contact with potential clients; you need to engage in a conversation with your market. If the time zones are weird or screwy, build a schedule that allows some overlap with US market hours and spend the rest of your day on product, engineering, and marketing. When making outbound calls, set up your call system so that a US phone number shows up on caller ID. Avoid Skype if you can, as I continue to have mixed results with that service. Nothing blows up a phone call like attenuation on the line.

Make it a point to do a minimum call count every day to potential customers, no matter what. Perhaps you can extend your day if you're based in Australia, Asia, or Europe to work in these calls every day. Nothing you do will replace selling to the right people in your industry. This doesn't mean cold-calling either. This means identify truly qualified individuals at your target accounts.

What's the best off the shelf sales process and management software I can use starting out as I begin contacting potential customers?

My first instinct is to say, "Use Salesforce!" While it is an off-the-shelf product, you will need to configure it to match your business and data entry requirements. Because of its vast capabilities, you can end up in a black hole. The upside of Salesforce is the ecosystem and plug-ins built on the Force.com platform. Most major email marketing products are now built to communicate directly into Salesforce. Again, the configuration issue and the expense will make this daunting.

Consider some of the freeware and cheapware out there that are less configurable but get you 75% of what you'll need for the first few years:

CRMs: Insight.ly, Highrise, Zoho, BaseCRM

A couple of important functions to look for in a CRM:

- Ability to copy outbound emails to a contact. For example, if you sent an email to 'bob@hotprospect.com' via Gmail, then you should have the ability to copy that email to Bob's profile in your CRM. This is huge timesaver.
- Ability to track opportunities in a pipeline report. You need assess your pipeline regularly, so your CRM should give you the ability to customize this pipeline report as needed to match your business.
- A good internal search engine. Once you grow from 100 to 1000 to 10,000 contacts, you won't remember everyone's name, but you will remember snippets of conversions and emails you sent. You should be able to search for contacts and content freely, not just by an individual's name or their company.

Note-taking & project management: Evernote, BaseCamp

- I use Evernote (www.evernote.com) during sales calls to type out notes while on the call. It is useful for grabbing screen shots as well. I keep a separate "note" for each client and just add notes over time. Then, you can email the note to yourself and use the 'cc' functionality I described to log into your CRM.

- I set up Basecamp (www.basecamp.com) projects for each of my client projects, providing them access as well. I set up Discussion Boards so that we can place communication around key topics in one place, e.g., "Training & Implementation" or "General Questions." Basecamp allows you to post files and has the email 'cc' functionality as well. This is a good tool to use even before you sign up a client. Once you have a serious opportunity, set up a Basecamp project and include all of the various decision-makers on the project. This helps with the smooth transition from "sales process" to "customer implementation", because you have been communicating centrally for some time. I also post invoices and contracts here so that everyone can easily reference them down the road. You'd be surprised how both of these files are either lost or missed in email communication (actually, you shouldn't be surprised).

Email Marketing: MailChimp, ConstantContact, Genius

- I personally use MailChimp (www.mailchimp.com) and love it. If you send fewer than 5000 emails in a month, the service is free. I've set up a simple template I reuse each week for my outbound communication. You can set up lists, or groups, of contacts, e.g., customers vs. nurture list vs. prospect list.

- I'm sure ConstantContact (www.constantcontact.com) has much of the same functionality.

- I've used Genius (www.genius.com) in the past because of their plug-in to Salesforce.

- Primarily, you want to be able to track who is opening and clicking on your outbound communication. Integration of this information is also nice to have, which is why I previously used Genius. This is also why many people use Salesforce as their CRM; each of these email marketing companies plug-in directly to Salesforce to track this information by contact.

Email & Storage: Gmail, Google Drive, DropBox, Box.net

Marketing & Customer Analytics: Datanyze, Hubspot, Marketo, Eloqua

- Datanyze (www.datanyze.com) is great for the front end of the sales process, especially if you offer a SaaS product. They can tell you what SaaS products are used by your target companies, and send you a notice when a new product is added or an existing one is dropped. For example, say you have a Marketing Platform Software to compete with Marketo or Hubspot. You can set up notifications to tell you when a target client adds Marketo to their website. Very nifty for targeting. *[Note: I have done some unpaid advising for Datanyze over the past year. I have no financial interest in the company.]*
- Hubspot/Marketo/Eloqua (www.hubspot.com, www.marketo.com, www.eloqua.com) are excellent marketing tools to track all of your efforts across social media, email marketing, and other. They can be overkill if you are in startup mode and only marketing in a very targeted way, say via outbound calls and email marketing. They all have outstanding free resources and webinars and if nothing else, follow them on Twitter and sign up for their newsletters.

Efficiency Tools: Synata, CardMunch, Pocket Notebook

- Synata (www.synata.com) is a cloud search engine. It allows you to search within all of your internal tools for information. Think Google for your systems, for example, if you are using Gmail, Dropbox, Salesforce, and Evernote at your company. Inevitably, information about your clients and sales interactions are going to be spread across notes, files, and emails, even if you are using the 'cc' tool and ardently log information to your CRM. Synata is a search box that allows you to search across all of these internal tools at one time. *[Note: I have done some paid advising work for Synata over the past year. I have no shares or long term financial interest in the company.]*

- CardMunch (www.cardmunch.com) is great for conferences and vents when you meet many people in short burst.
- Pocket notebook (the paper kind…). Go to OfficeMax and buy 5-10 small notebooks that will fit in your pocket. Keep one in your car, one in your brief case, one at your desk, and carry one wherever you go. These are great for writing down ideas and phone numbers. As much as there are software apps like Evernote, nothing beats a piece of paper in a pinch.

Sales Professionalism

Sales: How do you become a better sales person?

1. Be mentally and physically fit.

Subscribe to Audible.com. Listen to books about selling, business, and personal motivation. Read novels. Do Lumosity. Learn a second (or third or fourth) language. Write poetry. Become An Idea Machine.

Exercise. Exercise releases endorphins and endorphins enhance creativity. Find an event and train for it - a 10k, a half marathon, a triathlon, a long hike, a century ride. Your goal will coerce you into regular fitness and a healthy diet.

The right diet and exercise provides you with a consistent energy level throughout the day, week, and year. The phone rings less at 3:30 in the afternoon than at 9:30 in the morning because people are on caffeine highs in the morning. The more consistently you perform throughout the day, the more calls you will make and more creative ideas you will develop.

2. Be disciplined.

...to prospect while your big deals reach their crescendo.

...to call clients the day after, the week after, and the month after, and every month thereafter to insure you've exceeded their expectations.

...to send handwritten "thank you" notes after sales calls, to clients, to referrers, and to colleagues helping you along the way.

3. Be prepared.

Map out each and every sales call, voicemail, and presentation. Map out the path to revenue. Identify the Buyer Types at your target companies.

Consider every word and every slide. Ask if they really matter to the prospect?

Write down your "Top 3" must-dos for today, the week, the month, and the year. Remember the rocks-pebbles-sand-water lesson.[12] You're customers are busy. You're busy. We're all busy trying to get less busy, yet always getting busier and forgetting about our business. If you're not prepared, you'll be stuck being busy doing nothing.

"Never start the day until you know how it's going to end." - Jim Rohn

4. Be creative.

...in how you approach prospects.

...in how you ask questions.

...in how you present.

---

[12] An explanation of this lesson: www.youtube.com/watch?v=38U_rLLW-qM.

…in how you structure contracts, implementation, and renewals.

…in what problems you solve.

5. Listen.

Stop interrupting. No one cares what you think or what your product does. They only care about their problems and whether you can solve it.

Ask questions and listen to the answer. Really listen. Then, ask, "What else?", "How do you mean?" and "How so?" These are the salesperson's "5 Whys" to uncover root causes and decisions.

Here's why hotels purchase and install business centers. And it's not so they can charge you $0.50 per page for printing. Do you know why your customers are buying?

6. Be cool.

Customers will unload on you, because it's your fault your servers went down last night. Product managers, marketing, and sales managers will unload because you didn't charge enough, you didn't ask the right questions, and you promised too much. All of these people are part of the symbiotic sales ecosystem. Take leadership when opportunities are blowing up and share the glory when that big contract gets signed.

Remember, a signed contract means you are just getting started. Product implementation, customer happiness, and renewal decisions start today.

Read "How to Win Friends & Influence People" annually.[13]

---

[13]Special thanks to Jason Buberel, my former colleague with Altos Research and currently an Engineering Manager with Google for this idea.

7. Compartmentalize.

Sometimes life happens.

Sometimes you screw up.

Sometimes people screw you.

Sometimes you'll have a whiz-bang road trip and think, "Flying to Des Moines in January isn't that bad after all!"

Sometimes you'll be on the phone at 1:30 am from a Hampton Inn with your engineering team the night before your $3 million meeting, asking how you'll be able to sell that feature which does not exist yet to the decision committee you've been working for 11 months.

Sometimes you'll wake up in that Hampton Inn and ask yourself, "What city am I in?"

No matter what, always smile when you're in front on the client. Never carry over the last call, last conversation, and last meeting into the next. Unless you're riding positive emotions. Then, by all means, ride that wave to shore.

8. Be consistent.

Relationships drive high-value selling. While you spend hours and hours and hours and hours thinking about your customers, they only think about you when you call or meet. And, even then they're thinking about their families, their other suppliers, and what time they're meeting up with their buddies for Monday Night Football.

You need to be consistent with your clients, so they know who you are. Get a haircut every two weeks. Buy 10 light blue dress shirts. Change your socks after lunch. Develop a personal regimen and stick to it.

9. Add value.

Share ideas with your customers, even when you're not selling to them. Send them articles. Share your notes from the conference they couldn't attend.

10. Communicate.

Pick up the phone. Tell your customer what you're going to do. Tell your customer when you are doing it. Tell your customer when it's done. Tell your customers when you can't keep your promise as soon as you know and recommend options to them, even if it's with a competitor.

11. Be honest.

...about price and cost.

...about your product's capabilities.

...about implementation timelines.

...about customer service and support.

...about customer requirements and communication.

...about a competitor's product, especially if it's better than yours.

What do you need to know to try and become a SaaS Salesperson? Or is it just another sales job?

Every sales job is different. Your product is different, your target market is different, and your customers are different. Yes, selling is selling at its core, but would a hardware engineer tell you they have the same job as a mobile app engineer?

A few concepts I've learned specifically about SaaS sales:

1. **Cost matters more than price.** With most SaaS products, you're selling a workflow improvement or efficiency gain. It is essential to know how your client operates in their daily environment. Learn Anthony Tjan's "The Three-Minute Rule" (http://blogs.hbr.org/tjan/2010/01/the-threeminute-rule.html).

    The last time my team's Salesforce licenses were due to renew, I was annoyed at the price for our 12 seats (~$12k+/year). I can use Zoho for $25/month per user (or less), but I didn't switch from Salesforce to Zoho, because the pain I'd go through to convert our entire sales and customer service systems was far more painful than paying $10k.

    This is also the reason why no one is really using your product during the free trials, even after you've extended the free trial three times. They care more about switching costs than they do about the price of your software.

2. **SaaS is a non-rivalrous good.** There is no inventory, which means "limited time price discounts" rarely motivate the prospect to close (assuming your product features remain fixed), and often just annoy both your prospect and existing customers.

    You create urgency by developing a collaborative relationship with the prospect and helping the prospect articulate the value they will receive by taking action.

3. **Prospects don't want to see a demo.** Weird huh? Here's what I mean: No one is interested in how your software works. They are interested in how your software solves their problem.

    During your initial customer demo, never walk the prospect through every single click and feature. "Okay, so when you log in, here's your personalized home page. Now, on the left-hand navigation bar, you'll see the 15 functions available to you. Let's start with the first one…"

    Do your situational analysis, so you target the primary factors that will cause your prospect to make a decision.

Sales: What are the most clever sales tactics you've ever seen?

An honest person, a good product, and a great company.

If you are selling to enterprises, the decision process and criteria is too complex and memories are too long for "clever" to work. You may be able to push your way to an initial meeting, product demo, or proposal through cleverness, but if a company stands to spend $10,000, $50,000, $100,000 or more, rest assured that "clever" will not win a sale.

And when you use these tactics at the onset of a relationship, you begin from a trust deficit. A couple of examples to avoid:

"Hi Mr. Prospect. We're surveying purchasing managers like you to learn more about..."

... then using this as an opening for a sales call.

"We have a new product we're rolling out. We're not selling it yet, but wanted to get some feedback on a few user interface design decisions. Would you mind taking a look?"

... then using this as a means to do a product demo and asking someone if they want to be part of your beta program.

Establish your reputation by adding value to the prospect and presenting a clear value proposition for your product or service.

How many cold calls should a top notch salesperson make in a day?

The short answer is: it depends. It depends on:

- Who you're calling - C-level execs with gatekeepers, senior/mid-level manager, or individuals
- Why you're calling - "Dialing for dollars" vs. "calling to establish a business relationship"

If you are "dialing for dollars," I consider that telemarketing, not cold calling.

The examples below assume you are calling to establish a relationship and rapport, with the objective to initiate a longer term sales process that might take weeks, months, or even years to close.

Three (3) examples from personal experience:

1. Software Products: Higher Education Market

Call Target: University professors

Calls: 15-25/day

Call Objective: Establish relationship and set up product demo call for the next week.

Process: Because most professors have a department-supplied webpage and an online vita, there's a huge amount of information available about them, including classes taught, syllabi, research interest, office hours, and personal educational background. I then knew teaching styles and assignments from the syllabi and their research interest, making it easy to develop a questioning strategy for the cold call.

Call preparation for each call took about 15 minutes to read the online info available and write out a call guide, questions I planned to ask and how I expected to lead the conversation.

Separately, there was the voicemail script, should I get only voicemail, common in academia. But when you get them on the phone, they can be a chatty bunch. (Professors are teachers and they have less allegiance to a regular schedule, so if I asked the right questions, a cold call conversation could easily go 30-45 minutes.)

Finally, I personalized a follow up email, which was another 5-10 minutes per call.

An average day would be 15-20 calls. Calling 25-30 would be a big day, but it also meant fewer connections. It's far better to make 15 calls and have 4-5 substantial conversations than make 30 calls with 29 voicemails.

Each substantial conversation usually entailed setting up a custom sample course for the professor to view and scheduling a 30-60 minute demo call over the next few weeks.

This means after a few days of effective prospecting/cold-calling, my next few days would be full with demos. From 20 "cold calls", I usually scheduled 2-3 demos for a few days hence. Completing four demos in a day was full day with preparation, set-up, pump-up, and follow-up after. After 3-4 days of cold-calling, the next 2-3 days were full with demos. I might do 20 cold calls a day for 2 or 3 days, and then not do any for several days.

2. **Analytics & Research: Financial Market Trading Desks & Investment Funds**

Call Target: C-level executives, Managing Directors, Traders, Fund Managers

Calls: 20-25/day

Call Objective: Establish relationship and set up product demo call for the next week.

Process: Most targets have LinkedIn profiles. Researching their background and their fund would take about 15 minutes per call and then I prepared questions and an effective voicemail script.

Generally, the same outcome is sought as the first example, to generate interest and then set up a more substantive call for a few days later to look at sample data and research together.

3. Commercial Real Estate: Community Banks, Regional Banks, Credit Unions

Call Target: Operations & Planning Manager

Calls: 20 calls in 4 hours. 40-50 for the day.

Call Objective: Establish relationship and set up face-to-face meetings with our broker.

Process: This was pre-LinkedIn (2003), but banks posted their senior management bios, so that was a start. Then, I would research that bank in places like Business Journal for articles about mergers, buyouts, or new branch expansion. This would enable me to speak intelligently about their real estate and location needs.

How do you deal with competitive products in use when you are first trying to crack open a sale at a target prospect?

Throughout the course of my outbound calls, I constantly run up against a couple of the same competitive products over and over. Our product is definitely better (really, it is!), but the prospects usually have low to moderate motivation to make a change.

Start by asking what your clients like about their competitors. I'll repeat that because you probably think that's a misprint:

Ask what your clients *like* about your competitors.

This is anathema to what you hear from sales experts. Usually, you're told to ask silly questions like, "If you could change one thing about your current solution, what would it be?" or "What do wish your current product would do that it can't right now?" These questions immediately scream to the prospect you are fishing for a sales handle of some kind, any kind.

Instead, when you start the conversation in a positive way instead, you accomplish two important objectives:

1. **You build trust.** Nothing throws a prospect more than hearing, "Oh yeah. I see lots of people using Product XYZ. It's really good and has lots of interesting functionalities. What do you like about it?"

   Imagine what the prospect thinks about you when you tell them you agree about how good a competitive product is? All the while, they were digging in for the sales pitch and you go and ruin it by being agreeable. That's a professional approach to sales.

2. **You will learn EXACTLY why the prospect decided to buy the competitive product.**

They'll tell you something like:

"The whizz-banginator on it is really good. We use it all the time."

Then ask the client, "Is that the main reason you decided to buy Product XYZ?" They'll probably tell you, "Yep, without that, we wouldn't be able to use it."

Now, what if your product also has a whizz-banginator that's proven to be 10xs better? If the client likes Product XYZ's version, you know they'll love yours. You've now uncovered a sales handle for yourself using a positive approach.

You can also follow up with a question like:

"What else do you like about it?" or "Does everyone else here at your company like the whizz-banginator?"

The prospect might tell you:

"Funny you should ask. I'm the only guy here that actually likes using this thing." Or "Oh yeah, everyone loves it."

In either case, you are developing situational analysis by gathering information in this way. Taking the positive approach will enable you to learn much, much, much more because you built trust from the onset.

Or... They'll tell you:

"You know, actually we bought it because we thought their doo-hickie was really good. Turns out it's not as good as we thought."

Then, ask the client, "Oh that's interesting. I have had a few people tell me the same thing. How important is that functionality for your day-to-day work?

This line of questioning helps you uncover real needs for the client.

Here's a basic example:

Let's say your competitor has a reporting function that allows their users to print out a weekly PDF file, and because you asked this positive question – "What do you like about Product XYZ?" – the client tells you how great this PDF report is for their accounting team.

But… your product can produce reports on-demand, export them into Excel, and sync automatically with any accounting software system. It sure seems like your product is much better than Product XYZ, and sure seems like your product would make life easier for the prospect's accounting team. Before diving in and telling the prospect all about your version, you need to qualify it first and establish need:

> "You said accounting is using that report? How do they use a PDF – do they have to transfer all of that data from the report to their systems by hand?"

See where I'm going with this?

How do I deal with gatekeepers? I am calling executive-level prospects, and nearly all of them have some kind of assistant that always screens their calls.

Be nice. Always, always, always be nice. Speak slowly and clearly, and always ask for help.

Consider that a professional assistant is really good at their job. Just like the executive they support, they have worked at their craft for many years to earn their position. When I worked at Pearson Education, most of the executive assistants began as editorial or marketing assistants and rose through the company ranks, just like the executives.

Next, remember executive assistants are dealing with other executives, both at their own company and with vendors. To be highly proficient at their job, they must be the type of person who is resourceful and helpful. Use this to your advantage.

Here's an approach to consider when you ask for the "Mr. Executive" and "Mary the Assistant" tells you he's in a meeting/traveling/not available/out of the office, say this:

> "Thanks, Susan. You know, I'm not even sure if Mr. Executive is the right person I need to talk with. Can you help me out?"

Mary will say:

> "Well, I'll sure try."

Then you say:

"My company, ABC Marketing, helps other companies with their email marketing, and I wanted to talk with the person at your company that can help me learn what systems you are using now so we can see if our ABC product is even a good fit in the first place. Who would be the best person to talk with about this?"

Mary will say:

A. "Well, Mr. Executive is certainly the right person."

Then you say:

"What's the best way to set up a few minutes with Mr. Executive to talk about this? Can we do that together?"

B. "Send me an email with information about your product and I'll share it with Mr. Executive. If he's interested, he'll get back to you to schedule a time."

Then you say:

"Okay, thanks Mary. I'll do that. I only want to send information that's relevant to your company. Can you tell me what system you're using now and what in particular has been useful for your company?"

This helps you qualify the prospect and begin some situational analysis. If Mary seems busy or isn't interested in helping, then simply agree to send the email and give yourself permission to call back in a week to ask for more information.

C. "You should probably be talking with our Marketing Department."

Then you say:

"Okay, great. Who should I ask for in Marketing about this?" Write down their full name and ask for the spelling. Then, ask Mary to transfer you.

It's highly doubtful Mary will ever tell you, "We're not interested." And if she does, then you need to call Mr. Executive when Mary isn't there.

There are many more iterations of what will happen. The point is to use Mary and treat Mary as a resource, not a gatekeeper. Mary knows everything that is happening in the company.

Hiring & Managing Salespeople

Sales Recruiting: What are the biggest risks in hiring a salesman at your startup?

1. Hiring any salesperson too soon.

If you've yet to acquire paying customers, then it's too soon; you're still in Customer Discovery and Customer Development mode. And, while Customer Development really is sales, as the company founder it is vital you develop a sales framework that includes buyer types (e.g., Economic, Technical, Users) within your target prospects and overcomes common sales hurdles (e.g., legal, technical, price).

By hiring a salesperson without clear knowledge of how and why your target market buys, you have no means to hold your salesperson accountable. It is very easy to confuse and justify salesperson activity for business development. "Well… he's been with us for six months and while he hasn't closed any deals, he's making lots of contacts and doing lots of demos. This will create market awareness for us and when the product is finished, we can close these prospects." Wrong. It may be you've hired the wrong salesperson, and it may be you hired a salesperson too soon.

Without metrics from which to draw - pull-through rates and timelines from lead to customer - your decision to retain or fire a salesperson lacks any rigor.

2. Hiring a senior salesperson because you think they will bring a Rolodex of contacts and customers.

The purchasing decision in an enterprise sale is too large for any one individual to blindly purchase a new product simply because that executive has a relationship with your newly-hired salesperson. A Rolodex may provide an entry point in target accounts but will not lead to sales.

Read these posts from Mark Suster on Both Sides of the Table: http://www.bothsidesofthetable.com/on-selling/

3. Taking an incorrect approach to candidate assessment.

Unlike many technical jobs, you cannot test a sales candidate on their proficiency. Traditionally, you are reliant on their resume and interviewing skills. To overcome this challenge, use behavioral profiles such as Myers-Briggs or Zero-Risk.

I've used Zero-Risk (www.zeroriskhr.com). It is very good at providing you specific questions to ask in an interview, so you can delve into potential weaknesses or mismatches between the job task and the candidate's behavior. Every salesperson will tell you they are entrepreneurial, don't require heavy management, and they love the challenge. These behavioral assessments help you separate fact from fiction. Another option is the DISC Profile (www.discprofile.com). Both are well worth the investment, considering the cost of hiring the wrong person at your company.

4. Hiring "closers" instead of creative problem-solvers.

Closers don't know the difference between an objection and a product requirement. "Okay Engineers, if you just add this and this and that, I've got three customers that are ready to buy…" Creative problem-solvers assess the client's requests and look for opportunities to begin working together, even if in a limited way while product development continues.

Closers focus on closing the sale, not implementing a strategic process for your client.

Read Jason Lemkin's answer to, "What are the best questions to ask a VP of Sales during an interview?" here: http://www.quora.com/Startups/What-are-the-best-questions-to-ask-a-VP-of-Sales-during-an-interview.

5. Hiring only one salesperson.

If your business has reached a point that you are compelled to hire a salesperson, then hire two salespeople. This diversifies your portfolio of salespeople, should one not work out despite following all the rules to recruiting and hiring. This also provides additional data points to measure salesperson performance, not just against your forecast but against each other.

Hiring two salespeople provides you insurance in working with individual prospects. It is very common that a salesperson's and a prospect's personalities simply do not match up. By having a second salesperson, you can bring her into the conversation.

You may also find certain salespeople do better/worse with certain kinds of accounts or markets. Now you can align these accounts based in individual strengths.

Lastly, this will enable you to scale faster, assuming you hire two effective salespeople. Training and ramp up time, particularly in an enterprise sale setting, is long and laborious. It may be six months (or more) before you see your first deal close from your new hires. As a startup, your business will be drastically different in six months. What happens if you decide then to hire salesperson #2? You'll need to wait another six months to see the revenue results.

What is a reasonable first year quota for a new business salesperson for an outsourcing company?

I was recently offered a quota of $8k of recurring revenue per month in new business, each month, and assuming no churn. This amounts to $624k in revenue in year 1, and my salary is $60k. Is this realistic? Should my quota be related to my salary? The company has no other salespeople, but nearly half a million a month in revenue. I would sell services like providing outsourced customer support for companies. What is a fair and reasonable quota?

The base is $60k, and the incentive plan also includes 8% commission on my deals for year one, and 4% of any increase for year two, and 2% of any increase for year three. Also included is medical and a 401k after the first year.

Typical deal sizes can range from $1k per month to $100k or more per month. The average deal is probably $5-10k after the ramp-up period. I understand there is always churn and just assumed no churn to make the numbers easy.

I suggest scrutinizing the internal capabilities and external demand for your outsourcing services to raise your confidence that this is achievable. One concern is your first-year quota ($624k) relative the company's current revenue ($500k).

A few questions to ask:

- How did the company accrue the $500k? Is this one big customer and few small ones? Did the big customer arrive because of a referral or "friendly"?
- How long is the sales cycle? Did it take 3 months or 3 years to land the big customer? Does it take 3 weeks or 3 months to close the smaller $8k deals?
- Is there a general sales model that has been tested to earn these clients, or were they all random in their own way? Scalability is a big factor to moving from the initial $500k to the next $624k you are expected to achieve.
- What is the expected churn? Are any of the current customers grumbling at all about service and results?
- How have the price points been validated? The $8k/month could be more difficult if you are required to discount from

list price to achieve each sale, or could be easier if you find you can begin inching up the price because your existing customers are very happy. Does the price point cover the true costs of business? Is the company's business model economically viable?

- What happens to leads and territories when salesperson #2, 3, 4 are brought on board later this year or next? How will that affect your ability to achieve your sales targets?

Base salaries are designed to cover your cost of living and the commission plan is designed to reward a successful salesperson hitting their personal targets. As a general rule, I've established compensation plans so that hitting goals equates to doubling the base salary. The plan you described (8% of $624k = $50k) basically gets you there at target the first year.

I do like the 4% and 2% annuity payout structure, so you seek long-term relationships with clients instead of landing short-term wins for the immediate commission. Overall, it appears to be a sound plan with clear structure and a nice benefits package. Scrutinize the business model and ask yourself if this is a service you'll be bragging about to your friends.

For TONS of details about compensation programs, check out: www.compensatingthesalesforce.com. David Chichelli wrote an excellent book detailing 50+ compensation programs.

As a sales professional, what terms can I negotiate to protect myself from being fired just before I close a monstrous deal?

I am about to close an extremely large recurring contract that, based on my 10% residual commission structure, will increase my monthly income by 5x with my employer.

Assuming I continue to perform this way, it's definitely not in the company's best interest, and we get along really well, but due to the potentially great increase in my income with them they want to just let me go so they don't have to honor our contract.

How can I prevent this from happening in the future?

1. If you're worried about getting fired for closing a sale, get a new job.

2. If your employer set up a commission structure that is going to negatively affect the company by paying you, get a new job.

3. If you believe both you and your employer want you to remain employed, but the compensation structure is not viable, then initiate conversation with your manager. Tell him you are thrilled with the bonus structure and would like to understand how it is economically viable for the company.

    If your manager is unable or unwilling to show this to you, get a new job.

    If he does show you and the numbers shake out, then you shouldn't worry. But the fact that you are worried tells me you should get a new job.

When do growing companies usually create sales quotas?

Does it usually revolve around a level of revenue, number of salespeople, number of total employees, or something else entirely? Is there even such a thing as a point where companies usually implement sales quotas? If there were one thing that usually marks the point at which quotas are implemented, what would it be?

Quotas should be implemented as soon as possible, with the understanding by both sides that the quotas may change over a reasonable period of time (say every 6-12 months). If you make changes too frequently, you'll demotivate your reps. Calculate as best you can how much time was devoted to sales, examine conversion rates, total number of calls, and sales cycle length when the founder/CEO (you I'm assuming...) led the sales efforts to determine the initial quota levels.

Begin your quotas with the first salesperson, so that you can test your quotas and have a documented method for evaluating sales performance in case you decide to make a change. It's a huge decision to hire the first full-time sale rep, because you only have one sample of how sales are progressing. This is a reason I recommend hiring 2-3 salespeople if you are planning to hire salespeople for the first time.

Managing Quotas:

Be clear and transparent with feedback. If your rep isn't hitting quota and there isn't a clear path to achieve it, cut bait and find someone else. Don't justify the cost center with mind tricks like - "Well, at least I'm getting market outreach" or "I can always call those people back" or "He's filling our CRM with contacts we can email later in a marketing campaign."

Expect your reps to do their jobs, but don't assume it. Set up a monitoring system as well ("trust then verify"). Early in the process, consider setting monthly/quarterly objectives around the total number of accounts and total revenue run rate and let the rep determine the best course of action to reach these objectives. Run this process for a few months/quarters and then you'll have more specific metrics on which to base a hard quota. Sit in on calls regularly. Have your reps record calls for you to review later to assess performance.

Share the company's business model to illustrate how the quota fits into the larger growth plans of the company and where shortfalls equate to slower engineering and hiring, and, thus, slower product development. This hits home for every sales rep, because they'll consistently hear from the market, "Can you add this or that feature? If you do, I'll buy it."

Consider adding a "discretionary" quarterly bonus **for cases where you want to** reward a sales person's work but because of product development delays or technical issues implementing the sale, they weren't able to achieve their quotas. Heed caution, but it's definitely worth considering in the early part of your work together.

Be sure you can handle the upside payout in the event the rep blows out their goal AND protect against consequences of cancellations.

Finally, remember this: Whatever incentive program you develop is what you shall get.

Example: Selling $500/month enterprise software in which the commission structure pays the first month's revenue to the rep and 5% for the next 11 months of the subscription, your rep has a heavy incentive to close new customers but not necessarily retain them.

Here are a couple of Harvard Business Review articles on this topic:

- "The Science of Building a Scalable Sales Team" (Harvard Business   Review): http://blogs.hbr.org/cs/2012/07/the_science_of_building_a_scal.html.

- "The New Science of Sales Force Productivity" (Harvard Business Review): http://hbr.org/2006/09/the-new-science-of-sales-force-productivity/ar/1.

What tools and ideas do salespeople use to stay motivated and productive?

On the software side, check out "The Daily Practice" at http://tdp.me. This is an easy way to track the important aspects of your day, both related to your work and personal life.

On the "good ole' traditional" side:

- **Prepare a hard copy of your call list.** This will give a targeted list, so you aren't wasting time digging around in your CRM for the contact info of people you want to call next. There is 95% probability you'll get distracted while in your CRM with something else - another lead comes in, you realized you hadn't called so-and-so in a month, you see you forgot to include the URL of an account in their profile and decide to take two seconds to do that. These are all unnecessary distractions when you're focusing on hammering out successful sales calls.

- **Use Post-it notes so you can see your progress.** Develop a color coding system if you need to – green for calls that lead to a successful conversation, yellow for a contact made but without a significant or successful conversation, and blue for voicemails. Post these on your wall or window so you can see your progress during the time block. When you're done, use the Post-it notes as a check list of follow-up requirements for yourself. Whatever you chose, develop some sort of system that enables you to see the results of your daily work.

Take a picture and keep a visual log of your work over time. It makes for an interesting composite when you view your pictures from a week or months. The color codes will help you spot trends in your calling.

Post the pictures to a Tumblr account with a little note about your day. This is also a good way to track trends – how did you mental mood affect your calls that day? Or was it vice versa...?

- **Set up a reward system for yourself.** Once you hit five successful calls, reward yourself with a walk around the block. Hit five more successful calls and buy a deluxe coffee instead of your regular small drip for hitting ten successful calls in a day.

I bring my workout clothes and go to the gym or on a run after a call block. You should be too mentally tired to do anything terribly cerebral, so this is a great time to re-energize for the rest of the day and feel good about yourself.

Make a pact with your development team or office mates – tell them that if you make 10 successful calls that include at least three significant sales advances before noon, you'll take them to lunch. Believe me, whether your office mates work with you or not, they'll be pestering you to do more calls. Everyone likes a free lunch, even if it's a burrito from the local shop. Even better, you can make it a working lunch and go with a purpose and a topic to discuss.

My skillset is in sales and business development. For our new startup, is it best I stay focused on just that or should I be getting involved in other areas?

By nature of the start-up environment, and especially as a salesperson, you will be forced to acquaint yourself with every aspect of the business. Otherwise, you won't be a successful salesperson.

A few examples:

Product Management: As you're selling the product, you'll receive feedback from the customers/prospects you'll need to relay to the engineering and product team.

Learn how to write up product specifications, not just two line emails like, "The customer wants to have a better interface." Get a clear understanding of what the customers want and why and develop a clear summary for the product team. As you do this, you'll be speaking in the product team's language, which will accelerate product updates.

Technology & Engineering: In sales calls, customers and prospects will ask you, "how does it work?" While you don't need to get into the guts of how many servers you have and whether your software architecture is Java or Ruby, you should know these things to project authority and expertise. Though, some of these engineering decisions may end up being differentiators in the sales process when it comes to scalability and customization for the end client.

Customer Service: Sell the product, and support the client. That's a rule. With a start-up product, your customers are buying of the trust and confidence you've developed with them. When the product crashes (and it will), you're going to be the first line of communication to your company.

My suggestion: Schedule weekly or semi-monthly 30-minute "walks" with the managers and key developers in each area of the company. Get out of the office, grab a coffee, and talk. Bring 2-3 questions with you every time. The questions need not be about the product or the company every time. (I mostly talked baseball with a particular Data Engineer in our walks.) The objective is to build knowledge over time and a relationship with everyone, because you're going to need them, and you don't want to be just the salesperson. Find out what they are doing and why they are making the decisions they are.[14]

---

[14] Ibid. Thanks again to Jason Buberel.

What is a sales bounty or account bounty when talking about sales commissions?

This is usually used in context of a competitor's product or "takeaway" account. For a particular product or market, a product team or sales manager is seeking to unseat competitors so they will list the accounts where a competitor(s) are used, and offer an increased commission rate (a.k.a. "kicker bonus," "sweetener," "bounty") to the sales team.

The perspective on using bounties is mixed. Those in favor point to the displacement of competition and the entry into an account with the initial product leads to additional business within the account down the road.

But...

Bounties negatively change sales rep behavior, because you may find the sales rep:

1. Offering special pricing, so special that the deal's profitability is jeopardized.
2. Including "add-on" features for free that should be part of an up-sell, such as training or implementation assistance.
3. Ignoring other accounts and opportunities with equivalent (or greater!) revenue that could be gained more easily than focusing on the sales bounty.

Other negative effects of bounties:

1. They create infighting among product teams - one product team offers a bounty or kicker bonus for selling their product, the other product teams get peeved. Not all reps have the specified competitor in their accounts. When a product team targets a specific competitor to unseat, the sales reps that don't have that competitor to sell against but still close the account are left thinking, "What a second... I closed my account too. Why does Jane over there get a kicker bonus?"

2. Bounties can reward poor past performance. When targeting a specific account in which the company may have little or zero base business, other reps who have been selling successfully to their accounts for years think, "Huh... so I've been selling $10,000,000 of product to XYZ account and get paid standard commission, but Bob hasn't sold anything to account ABC in two years so now they're offering a kicker bonus?"

If you haven't noticed, I'm not a big fan of bounties. In the end, a well-developed commission structure, good product, and sound marketing and sales support should result in takeaway business without the extra push of a bounty program.

Should a first time Vice President of Sales at a B2B tech startup hire salespeople who can only work remotely?

No freaking way.

And, this has nothing to do with being a first time Sales Vice President - it's about company culture and efficiency. Everyone at a startup needs to be in the office to watch the company grind and grow.

Think about the organic conversation that occurs when an engineer hears a sales rep on a call:

Rep: "Well, Mr. Prospect. That's not a feature we currently support.."

Engineer: [Perking up, whispering] "What feature?"

Rep asks the Prospect to hold on just a second and explains the feature request.

Engineer: "I'll have it done by noon."

Rep: "Well, Mr. Prospect. I just talked to one of our engineers. He said he can have that feature ready by tomorrow if you're ready to subscribe... You are? Great! All I need is a credit card..."

Alternately, think about the engineers discussing bug priorities. They decide to drop #837 down in the list. The rep overhears and says, "I've had three more requests today for that bug fix..." The engineers decide not to drop that bug down the list after all.

Software-as-a-Service (SaaS)

How do you drive a "sense of urgency" when selling SaaS or enterprise software?

Companies like Gilt Groupe and Fab drive a sense of urgency around purchasing, in that, if you don't buy it today, it might not be around tomorrow. Car dealers often have "end of month" or "end of year" incentives. Are there similar strategies that work with enterprise software or SaaS sales? How do you keep customers from dragging their heels if they are on the fence about buying the product?

SaaS are non-rivalous goods.[15] There is no inventory or "last items in stock" for SaaS products. This presents a specific challenge in the sales process for these goods. Techniques like the example described above do not and cannot work in selling your software and data products.

What does this mean for your sales process?

1. You cannot use time pressure or the "takeaway" close, which includes limited availability or limited time pricing in most cases.

2. You must identify a specific pain or problem for your prospect your product will mitigate. Many times, the need is

---

[15] https://en.wikipedia.org/wiki/Rivalry_%28economics%29.

not obvious to the prospect, which means you must be adept in helping the prospect learn this need for himself.

3. Inertia is frequently your biggest competitor in SaaS and DaaS. "We've done it this way for a while. We like your software and we know our current system isn't perfect, but it works well enough." If you hear this from your prospects, it means the pain point you are addressing is not acute enough for the prospect to invest their time and money in making a change to your product.

4. "No decision" is a legitimate decision from the prospect's point of view. If you have a "no decision" prospect, then you don't have a prospect; you have only a lead. It is your responsibility to help this person discover a need big enough and strong enough to initiate changes to their daily workflow.

For more on this, check out the SalesQualia company blog for these posts:

- "The Scarcity Effect & SaaS/DaaS Sales" - http://www.salesqualia.com/2012/09/17/the-scarcity-effect-sassdaas-sales/

- Considering a price increase to motivate your prospect? - http://www.salesqualia.com/2012/09/14/considering-a-price-increases-to-motivate-your-prospects)

Generally speaking, are SaaS companies more likely to be successful starting with small customers or big customers?

A lot of fast-growth SaaS startups seems to focus on smaller companies first (examples include Salesforce, Hubspot, Marketo, etc.). However, doing a deal with larger companies seems to move the needle more than signing up a lot of startups. It depends on the business, of course, but is there a path that generally tends to be more apt to succeed?

Over the long run, you will want to overcome the Pareto Principle (a.k.a. "80/20 rule", http://en.wikipedia.org/wiki/Pareto_principle) in which 80% of your sales come from 20% of your customers. This places emphasis on diversifying your customer base, and in your case, this means diversifying among large and small enterprises.

Now, the secret is 80/20 not only applies to revenue, but also customer service (80% of customer service is spent with 20% of customers). Over time, you'll need to assess your support time allocation to determine where you can scale and where you're getting bogged down.

Develop a decent pipeline of both large and small companies and review it rigorously every week. "Decent" can mean as few as 5-10 small business opportunities and 1-2 large business opportunities. Set a rule for yourself: for every large customer added to the pipeline, add 3-4 small ones. Pretty quickly, you'll be able to assess which, large or small, are generating a higher ROI. Once you roll along with this process and begin engaging in the sales process, then you will be able to assess the segment that provides better ROI, which may not mean higher top line revenue once you factor in total cost of the sale.

Then, develop a scorecard to assess each segment that ranks the key steps of your sales process on a scale of 1-5 (1 = less work, 5 = more work for you). This enables you to assess your sales model and ROI to each customer segments. An example scale:

<u>The Sales Process (score 1-5):</u> Which of your customer segments require more resources during the sale? Bigger companies tend to have committees and multiple decision layers. Smaller companies may take longer to decide because of internal time constraints. Lower pricing and a faster sales process to smaller customers can also mean lower risk for the customer.

<u>Product Customization (score 1-5):</u> Which of your customer segments require more product customization (i.e., "Okay, if you just add these three features, then we'll buy...")?

<u>Implementation (score 1-5):</u> Which of your customer segments require more support at the time of product implementation? This includes technical installation, documentation, product training, and back-end customization they didn't tell you about during the sales process.

<u>Ongoing Customer Service (score 1-5):</u> Which of your customer segments require more customer support after implementation? This includes training for new users, retaining existing users, fixing product bugs, upgrades, and general usage questions. Maybe the smaller customers have more issues and questions on the fly and expect quicker resolution, whereas your larger customers are okay doing a weekly or monthly call to review pending items and new requests. Or vice versa... It depends on your market and customer personalities.

This scorecard will help you understand pitfalls and scale for both customer segments. Then, you can decide which of these your company's organization is best able to satisfy.

Yes, larger companies often have people dedicated to integration. However, those some companies will assume you have dedicated people on your end to do the same just for them. Depending on your product, you might find your smaller customers are less work on the service side and thus provide a better ROI for you over the long run. While it sounds good to land 1-2 whales, if these 1-2 customers consume all of your company resources, then you've just become a consulting company instead of a software company.

For example, at CoreLogic (where I work on their Advisory Services team) there are 5-6 individuals solely dedicated to sales and customer service of the largest accounts, such as the "Too Big To Fail" banks and GSEs (Fannie Mae & Freddie Mac). These customers expect the subsequent support levels when they make a million dollar purchase.

Previously, with Altos Research, I worked with GSEs and a few large investment funds as our largest clients. As a small company (fewer than 20 people), I was the primary contact for product sales, implementation, and customer service for all of our big accounts (with help from QA engineer and our CTO when needed for highly technical questions). Very quickly, this system placed a major constraint on my ability to develop new customers, as I was traveling regularly to these major accounts and fielding product questions weekly.

What is the best way to justify **ROI** for **40-50k B2B** software deal?

Determine which of the four (4) primary benefit categories your product provides to your clients. (Hint: It may be more than one but need not be):

1. Increase Revenue
2. Decrease Costs
3. Increase Efficiency
4. Decrease Risk

Then, match the benefit(s) to each "Buyer Type" in the sale:

1. Economic Buyer
2. Technical Buyer
3. User Buyer
4. Product Champion

Include opportunity costs of both USING and NOT USING your product. Help your buyers discover these (remember the old adage: "Telling is not selling").

For example, if you're selling a CRM:

- By having a CRM, how much time would be available for the sales team admin to prospect for new clients by using a CRM?
- What is the cost to the prospect in continuing to use spreadsheets, in terms of lost information and sales?
- How would sales timelines and forecasting become more accurate with a standard report that flows to finance weekly?

Once you've mapped this, a story will emerge on how to justify the ROI for your product to each. Consider the implementation costs to the buyer as well such as training, switchover from old process to new, and any related software or hardware upgrades necessary. Sell to each buyer accordingly and summarize your findings to the Economic Buyer. You now have your ROI.

SaaS Marketing: What are the best customer engagement strategies when it comes to product's adoption?

Here's a similar framework that was described in "Major Account Sales Strategies" by Neil Rackham:

1. Needs Analysis
2. Evaluation of Options
3. Resolution of Concerns
4. Implementation

The "Implementation Stage" is as crucial to the sale as finding a prospect and answering objections.

A few tips:

1. **Do not allow ambiguity in your free trials,** such as, "We want to see if it's better than what we have" or "We're seeing if it's easier to use." You must put metrics to the free trial. What constitutes "better?" How will the user know if it is "easier to use?" Is that measured by integration with their CRM, by time to develop a campaign, or something else?

2. **Assign a "Success Coach" to each account** (actual title used may vary depending on your market). This is a different person from the sales professional. The Success Coach is responsible for achieving specific milestones with the free trial user, i.e., uploading user data into the system instead of mock data and establishing a fixed appointment after 3, 7, 14 days of the free trial's start. If the free trial user is not willing to commit to these milestones or interactions, they probably aren't a serious prospect right now.

3. **Create a verbal contract with your free trial users,** including specific use cases, upload user content or data, and a fixed timeline for ending the trial.

4. **Develop a specific hypothesis that the free trial is testing.** For example, if you are selling an email marketing solution, the free trial must test critical metrics for email marketing campaigns versus existing systems, such as click-through rates or conversations to page views. The more specific, the better. By focusing on a single problem or issue, you are focusing the client on how your product solves a real problem they face.

5. **State a trial close.** "If the product meets these criteria, will you purchase the product?" If the answer is "no", then ask what other criteria will be used to evaluate the product, or what other solutions are under evaluation.

6. **Ask how the purchase approval process works, before your start the free trial.** Ask, "When you find the product meets these criteria during the trial, how does the purchasing process work in your company?" If the user doesn't know, then you have a major problem. If the user says, "Well, then I'll present to my manager to ask for funding", then you know you have another layer to the sale. If the user says, "If it works, you send Mary the invoice and she pulls the funding from my operations budget", then you know you have a decision-maker.

7. **Consider the true implementation costs,** such as related software or hardware upgrades, internal process changes, budget approval, and the tendency of large organizations to focus on sunk costs for current systems and products. You may be ignoring significant implementation hurdles. If your free trials are not converting, you may be focusing too much on the "User Buyer" and not enough on the Economic Buyer and Technical Buyer.

What is the best way to sell and market SaaS software to ISPs and Telcos?

The software would fit into the ISP support section and tools for help desk. My current approach has been to cold call directly.

This is 2012. You should never, ever be cold-calling anyone, particularly in an enterprise sale situation.

I took five minutes to Google "telecommunications customer service conference" and found several events posted here:

http://www.customermanagementiq.com/events/

Go through each event and their agenda/speakers. These are the people you need to contact, because they are senior managers, influential in the industry, and will be influential in their organizations. For example, check out this list of people:

http://www.callcenterweek.com/

Would you rather blindly cold-call a company or ask for Ryan Jessop, Sr. Manager of Customer Management Systems at Cox Communications? Here's his LinkedIn profile[16]:

http://www.linkedin.com/pub/ryan-jessop/1/741/449

More broadly, you need to map out your sales process. You won't be selling to a single person at each company. Instead, it will be a mix of direct managers, and then upstream and downstream. Upstream includes their managers and directors, CIOs, CTOs, IT managers, and legal advisors. Downstream includes daily users and their customers. All of these people are stakeholders in the sales and use of your product. Map it out and start elbowing around in each company now you know how to identify key people to call. (Imagine if you could put together testimonials from daily users and customers

---

[16] Dear Ryan, I hope you don't mind. You were selected at random. If you'd prefer to be removed from this book, just let me know.

calling into the telcos about their daily problems and how you system solves it.)

Once you have your call strategy planned, think about delivering content and contributing to the industry thought process. There are plenty of opportunities for blogging and white papers you can then use, both as follow-ups to recent calls and outreach to newbies.

What are the most effective strategies for marketing a financial data product, e.g., Bloomberg, FactSet, Capital IQ terminal, to banks, hedge funds or mutual funds?

For example: Online (email / SEM), offline (print advertising), attending conferences, cold calling, etc.

With Altos Research (housing data), because our data products are relatively advanced and unique, I would offer to run a sample portfolio through our analytics platform and review the results together with the client over a web meeting. We've found this is a much more effective way of maintaining control of the sales process and answering questions as they arise. Otherwise, your prospect may only glance at your product and when you finally connect with them two weeks later, they'll say, "Oh yeah, I looked and a few things weren't working for me", but can't remember anything specific.

Requiring a synchronous conversation to review the results measures the prospect's commitment. It's easy for a prospect to say, "Oh sure, I'll check it out. Send me a login ID." It's very different to require them to work and commit to a time to review results together.

A few other tips:

- **Avoid email as the initial point of contact.** Pick up the phone and ask questions. It's the only way you're going to define work flows, uncover needs, and then gain commitment to the next step in the process. Email should be a way to communicate between phone calls, not in lieu of phone calls.
- **Add value to your target audience,** whether that is a regular report you can send and track opens or a webcast of some kind. Unless you're adding value, you're irrelevant to them.
- **Do what you say you'll do.** If you say you'll call back on a certain day and time, do it. These guys notice. Stay on top of

them. Everyone's busy so you need to lead the process and don't be shy about this.

- **Learn how to leave effective voicemails**. Check out Salesbuzz: http://www.salesbuzz.com/free-demo. There are a few free recorded webinars there that are fantastic.
- **Don't expect to get onsite meetings at first.** You need to develop the process and show you have the potential to add value before you'll be allowed onsite. Everyone is too busy for a "stop-by" meeting. Be able to sell over the phone.

We are an early stage software company and our solution falls at the intersection a couple of broad categories, i.e, BI and Performance Management (as defined by Gartner - sigh!) and I keep getting asked by people about which category we belong to?

If you're sitting around wondering about how to market as an early stage company, you're being incredibly lazy.

As an early stage company, you need to focus on sales. The market will tell you what segment you belong based on their decision to buy your product or not. (In "Lean Methodology" terms, this is called product-market fit.) Buyers are not looking for you or any company by category. You need to find them.

My suggestion:

1. Develop a prospect list of at least 100 senior managers at companies in your target markets. Use LinkedIn, conference agendas, personal and professional networks to do this.
2. Create a value statement for each segment that describes the benefits of your product in their terms (i.e., does your product increase revenue, decrease costs, increase efficiency?).
3. Make sales calls and describe your value statement to these decision makers.
4. Measure your progress. What level of interest are these managers showing? Are you moving from an initial call to a, "Hmmm.... This sounds cool. Can I see it?" [good] Or are you hearing, "Um, yeah... send me an email and I'll take a look." [bad]

Engaging in the sales process also identifies key elements to your target segments, such as the decision process, the purchasing process, willingness to pay, budgetary constraints, and sales timelines. It will also indicate if you're any good at selling your own product. Marketing can never, ever do you this for you.

Once you develop your first few paying customers (not free or beta users), it will become more clear about which segment on which to focus. Even if you don't close any customers immediately, you'll have clear intelligence about which target segments are even interested in purchasing and using your product pretty quickly.

Now, go make some sales calls.

About the Author

Scott Sambucci is a Silicon Valley veteran, spending more than 15 years building sales processes, developing new markets, and creating technology products for two successful startups and two publicly traded companies. Throughout his career, Scott has sold educational products, software solutions, data services, and consulting engagements to:

- Top universities, including Duke University, Columbia University, and the University of Pennsylvania;

- Financial firms, including Wells Fargo, Bank of America, Morgan Stanley, and Freddie Mac;

- United States government agencies, including the Federal Housing Financing Agency, the Department of Treasury, and the Federal Reserve Bank.

Scott leads workshops across the country to help companies and individuals improve sales performance, including a workshop at the 2012 Lean Startup Conference and regular sessions with the Lean Startup Circle Meetup Group network. He regularly teaches university courses in Economics, Finance, Entrepreneurship, and

Strategic Management and recently received a "Faculty Member of Excellence" award in 2012. Scott has been interviewed on CNBC, NPR, and The Financial Times.

Scott is the Founder of SalesQualia and lives in Northern California. He is a three-time Ironman triathlete.

CONNECT WITH SCOTT

www.linkedin.com/in/scottsambucci
www.quora.com/Scott-Sambucci
www.twitter.com/scottsambucci
www.twitter.com/salesqualia
www.salesqualia.com

About SalesQualia

Improve Sales Performance. Sell More Stuff.

SalesQualia provides:

- Personalized advisory and consulting services

- Sales Coaching Programs

- In-person & Online Workshops

- Sales Productivity Applications & Products

Visit www.salesqualia.com to register for the "SalesQualia Insider Updates" – weekly articles, videos, and ideas to help you improve your sales performance. (Yes – of course, it's free to register!)

29878730R00090

Made in the USA
San Bernardino, CA
31 January 2016